VALLEY WALKING

VALLEY WALKING

NOTES ON THE LAND

ROBERT SCHNELLE

WSU
PRESS

Washington State University Press
Pullman, Washington

Washington State University Press
PO Box 645910
Pullman, Washington 99164-5910
Phone: 800-354-7360 Fax: 509-335-8568
© 1997 by the Board of Regents of Washington State University
All rights reserved
First printing 1997

Cover: *Mountains*, 1924, oil on canvas, by William Thomas McDermitt, collection of Washington State University Museum of Art, bequest of Ernest O. Holland.

Library of Congress Cataloging-in-Publication Data
Schnelle, Robert.
    Valley walking : notes on the land / Robert Schnelle.
        p.   cm.
    ISBN 0-87422-151-X (cloth.)—ISBN 0-87422-150-1 (pbk.)
    1. Natural history—Washington (State)   2. Natural history—New England.   3. Human ecology.   I. Title
QH105.W2S37 1997
508.797—dc21   97-269
                                                        CIP

For Lori

Ah, where have they gone, the amblers of yesteryear? Where have they gone, those loafing heroes of folk song, those vagabonds who roam from one mill to another and bed down under the stars? Have they vanished along with footpaths, with grasslands and clearings, with nature?

Milan Kundera, *Slowness*

Contents

IV

Invitation

We cannot go to the country
for the country will bring us no peace.
—William Carlos Williams, "Raleigh Was Right"

IT MUST BE ANCESTRAL, this longing for a landscape's embrace. Roman patricians repaired to their vineyards; Elizabethan courtiers sought the greenwood. Thoreau camped at a lake, Mary Austin homesteaded the desert, and John Muir waltzed among California's high peaks. Are we naive to wish for the same? The intimacy of trees and familiar flowers, the reassuring patterns of life among seasons fully experienced—these are no less our birthright than before.

But nature eludes us now. Yosemite is a parking lot, and Walden Pond rocks to the rhythm of the boombox. While our mountains recede ever more poignantly into the haze of auto exhaust, Wal-Mart claims every pasture. Once perceived as a healthy escape, the countryside disintegrates into fragments. If it's wilderness you want, that far-away refuge of rock climbers, apply for your permit in advance.

We have come to identify with nature through packaging. For many people, equipment fetishes or ecotourism appease the appetites once gratified by daily living. Others, myself among them, would sooner don a straitjacket than enroll for a gourmet rafting trip. High-tech athletics are beyond my ken.

There must be a way to come home; enter the landscape unencumbered; be content with witnessing. What if, despite the momentum of late capitalism—its smug assurance that land and people are commodities—what if we followed Edward Abbey's advice? Even now we could climb out of our cars, walk ourselves footsore (in concentric circles if necessary), but in the end let a patch of local terrain reclaim us. If the world looks diminished, look more deeply. I have tried to countenance my adopted home in a valley of the far West. But I am speaking of a way almost anyone may try, urbanites included. Distant national parks are inspiring places. Still, I'm searching for wildness in a state of mind. It comes to me when I step outside.

We are fallow fields after all, ripe for the seeding of volunteer growth. If the neighborhood watershed reclaims us, then we won't need to go to the country. We will already be there.

Robert Schnelle
Cattail Creek
Kittitas Valley, Washington, 1997

Part I

Snakewalk

G IVEN A CHOICE between inspiration and chilidogs, most of us will opt for lunch. The flesh is weak, and I am no exception to the rule. But life is not all one thing or another, and so the eclectic side is what I'm after when I walk in Umtanum Canyon, an east-west running gorge that slices through the heart of the Yakima drainage where I live with my family. We fill our daypacks with pickled herring, mushrooms in garlic sauce, and all the chocolate peanuts they will hold, then we make tracks into a pocket of wildness a dozen miles from town. There we find birdsong and creek rills tippling through a sleeve of greenery. Cottonwood and aspen groves, beaver dams, bunches of purple monkeyflower appear. And high above them all rise weird, basaltic rock formations as yet unknown to the makers of four-wheeler ads. These surroundings beckon the walker to take it easy, but take it.

My wife, Lori, our baby boy, Erik, and I forded the Yakima River on a cable-slung footbridge, clomping like billy goats gruff above the heads of rubber-shod anglers flicking trout wands. We crossed a section of the Union Pacific Railroad and found our trailhead in a thicket. Locals have dubbed the canyon "Rattlesnake Alley," but our little party agreed at the outset to savor the whiff of danger. Counting on vibration to warn of our approach, I beat time with my walking stick while Lori winnowed the grasses with a branch. Erik rode snugly on my shoulders. When he learns to speak he can call me Papa. For now, strapped to an expedition-weight ten month-old, I call myself Sherpa.

At a half mile we emerged in a meadow of sage. Lit by the morning sun, plumes of rabbitbrush let the earth say, "Autumn." Vine maples and golden willows spoke their piece beyond. In prairie country it is especially good to look at trees as tall companions, quiet guardians converting solar energy to food, who transform their leaves to fire at year's end. In fact, however, botanists know that the fall colors have been present since springtime. This Lori confirmed by quoting from our field guide as we walked. The brassy hues of cottonwoods, she explained, expose themselves only when their chlorophyll's green begins to fade in September. "Why here, then," I asked, "do aspen leaves always turn *yellow* rather than orange, say, like the leaves of Douglas maples?" We learned that this is so because they contain huge amounts of a pigment called xanthophyll. The umbers, ochers, and reds of other trees derive from chemicals equally worthy of intonation in a Gregorian chant: *"Tannin-carotenin-anthocy-a-nin!"* we sighed. Even after the leaves flutter to earth, however, they play an inspiriting role. As everyone knows, leaves make topsoil, and until the snow falls, they would protect this ground from eroding winds.

Like the cadence of the seasons, our pace found the rhythm of some unseen, geophysical clock. The day began to warm. We took sit-downs every half hour or so to accommodate Erik, Lori pouring cider from a thermos while I helped him stretch his legs. He likes to grasp my bony fingers in his pudgy ones and pace out spirals in the dust. The footprints he leaves appear aimless, but I intend to study them one day, suspecting they will trace out the algorithm for a walker's golden mean.

By late morning the trail had begun to turn back and forth, braiding itself across the brook repeatedly as if to improve our chances of meeting a water-seeking reptile. "Sinuous," "serpentine," "snakelike," and similar words occurred to me later, though it was right then that the dust ahead of my feet coiled up and reared. Here, after all, was a rattlesnake. Too young to make much commotion with its tailpiece—and still too sluggish from the pre-dawn chill to beat it—the snake had to confront us in the most sincere fashion it knew, roiling its tiny head and hissing like a teakettle. Just a fingerling of fear with a pink mouth. I thought it was the most innocent creature I had ever seen, but Lori's genes told her otherwise. Her revulsion at the snake's dry-bones rattle suggested some primordial imprinting that I myself seemed to lack. We held our distance until the snake slid away.

At least as interesting as human phobias is the evolution of the rattlesnake itself, especially its well-known audible feature. According to the naturalist Janine Benyus, one theory about rattles states they were meant as a warning to predators, who, like the snake itself, would stand little to gain from a high-risk confrontation. A second hypothesis holds that rattles are alarm signals designed to keep bison from trampling the legless. Yet another idea is that the snakes evolved rattles to lure victims into striking range. Whatever the case (and I don't see why it shouldn't be all three), the western rattlesnake is deaf to its own rhythms. Without the benefit of ears, the only things it hears are earthborne vibrations transmitted through the spinal chord.

The sun at its zenith hung low this time of year, but glances of sky above the canyon looked bluer than in summer. We ate cheese sandwiches on a log. I could see the creek spinning itself into whirlpools while waterstriders—those elegant, surface-riding bugs—began to circulate in eddies. Erik mouthed an alder cone. Beside him, Lori read aloud from our field guide. It turned out that snakes don't need ears. Like all pit vipers, they've got heat sensors between the eyes and nostrils by which they can take infrared soundings. Even in darkness, when a pack rat or a human ankle appears close by, it looks "hot" to the snake, who then calculates the object's distance for an accurate strike. On our feet once more, we tapped along cautiously. I tried a syncopated tempo as a gesture of appreciation for whoever else might lie concealed.

Umtanum Canyon rises gently as you hike, and the landscape crumbles and reconfigures itself en route. Before you know it you are far in. We welcomed the sense of going deep that you get in a canyon hike. We welcome it anywhere for that matter, the hope being that by leaving constructed places behind we might glimpse another world, a scene of fresh possibility. Perhaps, I thought, as noon gave way to nap time, it is their otherworldliness that accounts for the beauty and terror of snakes. For centuries they have graced American rituals from Oraibi to Appalachia. Physicians preside over deaths as well as healings, and they, too, claim the serpent as their totem. We now inspected the ground for totems where the south rim of the canyon dissolved into broken slopes. Satisfied, we paused for another go at lunch. The spot was christened with campfire rings and grasses palatable to bighorns. We fingered heads of wild rye, grandmother to the grains baked in our sandwich bread.

Walking out again, I composed the day in my mind: a morning ripe with fall, a child bending ancient stems, and a snaky footpath just far enough from the manicured lawns of town. These would suffice to keep body and soul intact.

Back to Nature

Vladimir: (impatiently). Yes yes, we're magicians. But let us
persevere in what we have resolved, before we forget.
—Samuel Beckett, *Waiting for Godot*

ONCE UPON A TIME, nature was a harmless topic. Like interest rates or carburetors, nature could absent-
mindedly break the ice in mixed company. The
subject held no linguistic pitfalls. Wholesome trivia about songbirds had little to do with the rough stuff of grown-up talk.

For many in the 1960s, "conservation" was a matter en-
trusted to summer day camps. Like all the sensitive kids who
didn't drive power boats, my sister and I, along with a dozen other
kids of conscientious parents, would spend our mornings in July
fanning out over Cape Cod clam flats. In tidal pools we harried
fiddler crabs, and then, settling our karmic debts, we would take
flight from biting sand fleas, hollering like refugees from the
planet Dune. My friends and I netted leopard frogs in murky
backwaters. We let painted turtles languish in aquariums. With
my mind's eye I can see our counselor, Mr. Finch, a stork-like figure with sun-bleached eyebrows and ace binoculars, as he holds
at arm's length a castaway goosefish, exclaiming, "Here is a *very*
interesting species."

In the sixties, few among the adult public gave nature a second thought. If they did it was only to approve of children's books
featuring rabbits. Others, like Mr. Finch, found in nature objects

to appreciate or to study in scientific terms. But nature lore honed no edges. Our counselor seldom took risks with emotion, there being little reason to flap. At mid-century nature was a backdrop where even pollution could be considered a darned nuisance. "No swimming today, children. The lake is on fire." After all, the moon was about to be conquered. Natural resources were conveniently harvested for the good of our living standard, biologists had classified the creatures worth knowing about, and serious people could anticipate the dream of cyberspace.

Need it be said that our views have changed? I can't pinpoint a moment when the big tree fell that broke the forest's back, nor when the plankton expired that told us we'd rattled the food chain. When, for that matter, did drinking water start metastasizing in our cells? The world as we imagine it is now, once again, understood to be fatal, and nature has become a prickly topic. So often it's about people's jobs, family planning, or consumer choice—private matters with planetary effects. No one questions whether nature merits discussion. It's all we have, though by this recognition we come by our ambivalence.

Time magazine proclaimed the news a few years back when it named Earth the "Planet of the Year" and nature the year's top story. I don't know what superlatives *Time*'s editors have chosen since, but I find myself blushing at such oracular prescience. Paging through that magazine, I felt like a government-schooled Indian reading of Columbus's windfall. O brave new world.

Yes, kicking and screaming, we have gone back to nature. Third graders unacquainted with local woodlands can recite surprising facts about the Amazon. In my town, some of the most avid recyclers are seniors, perhaps nostalgic for their days of wartime thrift. Even middle-aged professionals feel the occasional flutter of conscience while burning gas to rent a video or quashing take-out containers by the pound. If nature has reacquainted us with guilt, we wonder, can repentance be far behind? Is the revolution of consciousness at hand?

Unfortunately, we look to national leadership in vain when seeking avatars of change. According to one congressional demagogue, environmentalism is a smokescreen for "ecosabotage" of the American economy. A popular talk-radio lout refers to the Audubon bird count as a rite of "pagan tree worshippers." Yet, disgusting as it is, such rhetoric spellbinds as often as it offends. Unfettered by any petty regard for truth, pseudo-populists have so mastered environmental debates as to have them both ways. When suitable, they incite the God-fearing against heretics in Gortex, and then when convenient, they assure moderates of their respect for science. An ad for a foresters' council promises, "We care! Northwest forests are healthier now than ever before." Next to an illustration of smiling family members hiking under old growth, we read that "there are now *more trees* in the Northwest than there were a hundred years ago." Yes indeed, thinks the skeptic, and if a few more of those trees exceeded ten inches in girth, we might be speaking a common language. Not that politicians and timber executives are the only ones doctoring words. Heralding the Ellensburg Rodeo parade a few years back, a Cadillac bursting with Stetson hats carried a banner emblazoned, "Kittitas County Cattlemen's Association—Stewards of the Environment."

Lately, doublespeak has veiled even more naked forms of destruction. A Southern congressman pledges to restore "balance" to farming regulations by legalizing the deadly pesticide, DDT. In sympathy, a senator from Texas argues, "There's something more important than the environment, and that's freedom." Without pressing for clarification, we can hear in America's anti-enviro discourse an absurdist's patois. Polls taken during recent years show that 70 percent of citizens consider themselves amenable to environmental protection, among us a healthy swath of Texas voters and agents for half the earth's resource consumption.

Awareness, if not behavior, has undoubtedly changed since the 1960s. Back then, exploiters lost as little sleep over the Sierra Club as over the fate of Esperanto. Birdwatchers, though lathered by the prophecies of *Silent Spring,* could still walk solitary beaches. There among the dunes, egg clutches of piping plovers might as yet be found uncrushed by offloading jetskiers. Caution was a matter for the future.

Now, with our future withering on the bough, Americans aspire to good behavior—whatever that is. So long as it doesn't touch our investment income or impinge on our fun, environmentalism sounds practical. Recycling, for instance, is a worthy practice, but reducing use we're not so sure about. Here in Washington, orange juice trucked from Florida outsells local apple cider. Ballooning square footage guides the middle-class housing market, while backyard burning is still "a way of life."

Yet, worrywart that I am, I recognize signs of progress, too, and anyway, it is self-defeating to abandon minority wisdom just because it hasn't caught on. Sooner or later necessity will sway the ruling powers. Of course, no one looks forward to change wrought in extremities, and I wish that my neighbor's xeriscaping were already civic policy. It would delight me no end to see cold-weather bus service for my bike-riding colleagues, the federal tax code revised to encourage small families, and wild habitats respected as we respect the authority of property lines.

But until a genuine land ethic takes hold, I will have to honor it in the play of my son, who haunts remnant marshes looking for leopard frogs—and other very interesting species.

Ingalls Way

"BEAR US IN MIND" suggested the sign depicting two large animals, the black one and the hump-backed grizzly. But we had counted two dozen hunting camps along the final stretch of Teanaway Road. The odds of our meeting with a bear looked poor.

Ingalls Way, the high route that promised to lead us to a tarn of the same name, begins in thick woods. We smelled the nutmeg odor of Douglas fir and the grapefruit scent of grand fir. Both dripped frosting from the previous night. Snow we could see on the summits had turned to frozen sleet below, so we settled our hat brims to shed the drizzle. The trees thinned out soon enough, their cover broken by meadows, and before long the sun appeared and we were climbing a slope studded with outcroppings of obsidian. I cracked off pieces of the glassy stuff, whose keen edges recommended its use for arrow points and spears.

At the juncture with a trail to Long's Pass we rested on a carpet of kinnickinnick, which is the spicy Algonquian word that signals a generous, berry-bearing plant. Birds eat the berries and so do bears. From there we looked yonder at a colony of club moss. These fern relatives resemble miniature hemlocks, palm trees, or junipers—anything but moss—yet long ago in the Triassic period, they formed the canopy of giant forests. Long-necked sauropods once browsed their greenery. Now, though shrunken to a present height just inches from the ground, they maintain their original shape. I can't help thinking that humanity's future, if we have one, lies in similar acts of modesty. Bears are immodest, but then they don't overbreed.

Ingalls Way climbed next to a terrace of wind-sculpted, whitebark pines. Through an arch of these krummholz we could stare at the presence of Tahoma, or Mt. Rainier as we white folks call it. Nearby vistas took in the sawtoothed Esmereldas. Up and over a saddle we hiked before dropping into a cirque where bogs percolated at the source of Ingalls Creek. Colonies of pikas emerged from boulder fields beyond. They traded calls as we approached; one of them dropped its mouthful of hay to watch the parade go by. We crossed another pass and scrambled to the shore of Ingalls Lake, a cradled dish of skywater overshadowed by Mt. Stuart, and an austere retreat at 6,500 feet. But when we arrived it seemed to breathe tranquillity. Sunlight turned the shallows a cool jade; in shadow, they reflected perfectly the cliffs that immured the lake. Only snow crumbling underfoot broke the stillness of the place. At last we spread our tarp and stretched out to watch the clouds. From clumps of dwarfed tamaracks, golden needles sifted.

Mountains being harsh and unpredictable, we didn't fret when a squall appeared, not straight off at any rate. When rain pelted our faces, though, we acknowledged the doubts that turn you back on a round-trip excursion. For sublimity, nothing compares to alpine landscapes. Yet they stir a sense of things forbidden. Watching clouds veil the glaciers of Mt. Stuart, I thought of Lord Franklin marooned on an ice floe. I remembered Thoreau's panic when lost in the fog on Mt. Katahdin: "Contact! Contact!" he scribbled. "Who are we? Where are we?"

Back below timberline, signs of our native elevation reassured us. Even now, in October, streams and woods gave the mountain an intimacy that spoke of refuge. We heard the unseasonable call note of a varied thrush. A pair of whiskey jacks bolted from the ridge as though slingshot. Even the rain felt friendly here. I unzipped the front of my anorak, where my little Erik had taken shelter from the wet.

When people who know about danger speak of "palpable" fear they are merely being accurate. As I rounded the next switchback and heard a loud, tooth-gnashing growl, I felt ice picks tickle my scalp. Adrenaline moves more quickly than a stalking predator. I found time to scan the woods for a scrambling tree, but the bear that was about to appear didn't show. Inside my anorak Erik snored and ground his newly sprouted molars, a yearling cub in a faux marsupial pouch.

After a while we saw the profile that marks the parking lot. Viewed from eastward, Esmerelda Peak shows a round-headed troll jutting from its southern slope. On moonlit nights it is said to resemble a bear.

Family Tree

Mantis

S HE CAME TO US in September. Captured live from our neighbor's hayloft, Artemis showed a catlike refinement. We spent several days watching her groom. Stretching one forelimb to scratch behind the place her right ear would be, if she had ears, she would then scratch behind the left. I know of no other creature in her tribe that turns its head, but Artemis turned hers from the food we offered. Spiders, houseflies, case moths—nothing seemed to please her. Then, one evening at twilight, Artemis tore the thorax off a grasshopper.

Artemis is the first green predator we've entertained in our house. She's got long, green pinchers; green almond eyes; an egg-laden abdomen tapered like a willow leaf; and retractable green wings. She likes to hang upside-down from a twig. Artemis is a praying mantis. To live with her, though, is to want to deny her kinship with earwigs. Most arthropods are crawling, fluttering, or scuttling things. A mantis is a tiger on six legs.

Watch Artemis stalk her prey with me: crouching motionless on a ficus twig, she spots a cricket deposited in her cage. Slowly the leg joints give in sequence; now the spiky forelimbs gather. Eluding the cricket's notice, our hunter closes the distance from her quarry with slow, silent skill. Then, for a moment, like a batter at the plate, she weaves in anticipation. Quicker than eyesight she darts to the kill. For twenty minutes thereafter we observe the denouement of a carnivore. She buries her face in the victim. She devours the cricket alive.

My high school biology teacher, a Jesuit, decried the praying mantis as a hypocrite of the insect world. Like St. Jerome, he preferred the work-a-day honey bee. I suppose I had already heard the witticism back then about praying on your knees every Sunday and preying on your fellow man the other days of the week. So I didn't get too alarmed about bug bigotry, even when Brother St. Pierre grew red in the face describing the predatory advantage of the mantis's prayerful stance. Perhaps it did remind him of sinful humanity.

Subsequently, I have learned that predator aversions like Brother St. Pierre's are not limited to insects. Hatred of claw-bearing animals has been a national pastime of sorts, one that has engendered a century-old campaign to empty the West of "vermin." To this day, our taxes fund the Agency of Animal Damage Control in its work to erase the coyote, the bobcat, the lynx, and the mountain lion. Wolves, eagles, grizzlies, and wolverines were casualties of yesteryear and are now largely absent among native fauna. Wherever people have sought exclusive rights to land or to game herds, their hunting competitors have been trapped, shot, or poisoned until locally extinct. Still more devastating than these weapons, of course, are the developer's bulldozer and the hill-climbing skidder.

If the praying mantis has escaped censure outside of biology classrooms, its habits and size have helped. Compared to a mantis, the evasive cougar is downright conspicuous. Probably, though, these insects prevail because they eat what we don't, including bugs that eat what we do.

Public indifference to biocide in all its forms will cease only when the delight that fosters a sense of kinship is felt. That's why I keep Artemis the praying mantis in my kitchen. Admiring the expertise of this creature, I believe I am learning my family tree. Anyway, whatever odd hobby works is worth a try on this page in history.

Owls

As weighty and self-contained as an old tomcat, but more fierce by far in bill and talon, a great horned owl dozes away the morning in our willow break. At first we watch it eyeball juncos pecking millet seed in the grass. It preens a while, then draws up a robe of feathers and seals its twin yellow orbs. From the vantage point of our kitchen window the owl looks formidable. With that creature on watch, I will outfit my toddler with a bicycle helmet before he goes out.

I like to think about the great horned because it lives everywhere in North America, and so it reminds me of my family's scattered origins—my young son's Washington, my wife's Minnesota, and my own New England. As we grow accustomed to the wide Northwest, we look to the animals and see what they do.

For one thing, owls are wild—they don't cross continents for better jobs. We can't explain them in human terms. Many of us first know owls as the pets or victims of taxidermy that turn up in natural history museums. There they perform compass turns of the neck or crouch unmoving, stiff as pine bark. Owls in the woods navigate thickets impenetrable on foot. They stalk on silent wings and seize a dozen mice in a night of hunting. A woodsmen's maxim holds that when a pine needle drops to the forest floor, the deer will hear it, the bear will smell it, and from a mile away, the owl will *see* it. According to my neighbor, Joe Powell, the great horned owl deals death to the red-tailed hawk by beheading this enemy and devouring its brains. Some tribal Americans hear fate in the owl's call, but these brave birds also brood their clutches in winter and so bring life to the cold. Once, after locking eyes with a great horned owl in my mother's ash tree, I decided to walk across Europe. Owls can't help their significance.

Yet all else being equal, owls mean more to Northwesterners than to other people. Not that raptors are more numerous or closely observed around here. It took the creation of a symbol to bring owls out from the woods and onto the region's tee-shirts. Spotted owls are thought to be the least assuming of their kind, undeserving of puppy love and scapegoating alike. But west of the Rocky Mountains, emotions gallop when you talk about ancient forests.

Coming out from Vermont, my family has learned to do without old standbys like hardwood trees and restraint. And we have thought half in earnest to apprentice ourselves to the great horned owl. There it is roosting now, for all the world as robust as a wolverine. That burly chest. Those head lamp eyes. The rep for inscrutability. Here is a creature fully itself and in place. There are worse teachers for an immigrant seeking home.

Coyote

No one who's ever been deflated by a jaw-cracking yawn needs to be told he is boring. But the rules change as we move among species. Bears yawn when they mean to do you harm. Lion prides, on the other hand, will gape open-mouthed as an exercise in solidarity. According to the naturalist Will Curtis, the crocodile's yawn invites the services of teeth-cleaning birds, daring symbionts who exchange their dental expertise for a meal. Finally, however, it is only the coyote that yawns out of insouciance.

Credited by some with fixing the constellations in the sky, coyotes are also known for their Houdini-like elusiveness. Nobody melts into grass like fox-eared *Canis latrans*. Watch him loping over the barrens at daybreak, casting around for a game trail. A circle-about here, a double-back there, then at last a tack is taken, the song dog's head lifted only to fix its bearings on nearby hills from time to time; otherwise it keeps nose to the bitterbrush. Then all at once, olfactory alert stops it short and brings the coyote eye to eye with a man, the latter peering through binoculars. Before the man's lenses are properly focused that rounder is gone. Rather seize a smoke ring than track the coyote.

My own first acquaintance with coyotes goes back to a wooded hollow in Vermont. Rains came hard that fall, and I was out inspecting salamanders at about the time when Jack-in-the pulpits bear their peppery fruit. The tree canopy staggered under the latest downpour; mosquitoes whined at my temples. So it was I heard no other hubbub until the hobblebushes exploded in my face, and there stood Old Man Coyote, big and toothsome. We two locked eyes long enough that later I thought some greeting must have passed between us, though in fact, Coyote had backpedaled and cleared two mountain ranges before my shout was lost in a thunderclap.

Lest you think me jumpy—coyotes being shy and harmless overall—it is a fact that their eastern cousins are larger than our western friends. Migration north of the Great Lakes may explain this fact, the genes of wolves possibly having mixed in to account for the sole carnivore that gains stature as you travel eastward. There, as here in Washington, coyotes glean much of their living from surplus deer and rodents; one gunned down for trespassing had his stomach opened to reveal a horde of grasshoppers. But do we love them for their part in the web of energy exchange? We do not—we kill them, prompting female survivors into estrus, so that more pups are born and their numbers keep healthy.

Speaking of battles, the conflict of the decade in our valley is waged over land use. Where some assert rights, others call for responsibility. Oddly, no one calls upon Coyote to mediate. Yet by force of experience, coyotes are best qualified to show the difference between land and other forms of property. Inquire of Coyote why land will not stay put behind those survey markers. Polluted water and marsh hawks come and go; likewise pollen or smoke from a brushfire. But a sight that truly thrills is a Coyote vaulting a five-foot fence from a standstill. They know what to do about "property rights" and they do it with panache, one leg raised horizonward, yawning transcendentally despite the steel traps we muster against them. Coyotes will be combing this range in a thousand years. Yippee-yi-o-kiyay!

Starlings

Have you ever felt the sky darken above a feedlot or an urban park and had to block your ears against the screeching of a thousand harpies? If so, you can thank William Shakespeare for the privilege. During the 1890s, the American Acclimatization Society introduced to our continent every bird mentioned anywhere in all of Shakespeare's works. Their most successful immigrant was the European starling.

Like many creatures that have adapted to life around humans, the starling inspires little affection. It belongs to the guild of opportunists, as do we, meaning that it specializes in gluttony and in stealing habitat from others, partly by cleverness and partly by force of overbreeding. In the estimation of one expert, North America is home to three starlings for every house cat we keep. This is a bird that fouls its own nest and suffers epidemic plagues. It broods more eggs than it can support, sometimes three clutches in a season, consigning excess hatchlings to their fate. Starlings dwell in cavities hollowed out by woodpeckers or hammered into place by roofers. During wintertime, they form colonies that may number a hundred thousand birds, and they roost in such densities as to topple tree limbs. Aggressive males enjoy heat and safety at the core of these roost gatherings, but younger females are pushed to the outside edges. And while few animals besides humans kill others of their kind, starlings become murderous when competition for nest sites is fierce: the bird kills by digging its claws into an opponent's eyes and piercing the brain. Such violence exerts no appreciable check on populations, however. My family has seen what appear to be hybrids of the starling and the Western meadowlark at our feeders, and if anything, these show more assertiveness than either parent species. So it only remains to see whether they themselves can breed and conquer the world.

To watch a gang of starlings feed is to witness their awesome potential. No bird uses its bill more deliberately, its every stab in the weeds yielding some edible grain or insect. According to the ornithologist William Beecher, this is because the starling's jaw muscles are structured in order to spring the bill open rather than to hold it shut, and so the bird can thrust aside plants and seize its prey with a single stroke. In addition, the eyes move forward as the bill opens, granting the scavenger simultaneous binocular and myopic vision. Indeed, keeping fed presents fewer challenges than pestilence to a bird blamed for passing disease to humans. But let even viruses do their worst, the starling survives to stuff its crop with victuals and breed.

If only biology would foster the fair as well as the ravenous, we might have more bluebirds coexisting with family Sturnidae. Such a world would smile on the doomed African cheetah even as it might on our own quarrelsome kind. But in evolution, beauty is a hostage to change. Unscrupulous persons know this and distort the fact to justify their destruction of forests and waterways. They ignore the counter principle, that in the long run, nature always favors diversity. Starlings may now exert a friction against that rule. But their numbers would rapidly shrink if ours did, once native trees reclaimed the grain fields and all those mountains of cattle feed and human garbage disappeared. In the meantime, we might as well admit their virtues. Like people, even starlings are not an indubitably bad lot. Every species has its own beauty, an insight recorded by W.H. Auden when he vowed to make human thought

> ...alive like patterns a murmuration of starlings
> Rising in joy over the wolds, unwittingly weave.

Similar to William Shakespeare, the starling is also a vocal artist. I have heard their spiraling wolf-whistles gladden otherwise grim cityscapes. Ancient Romans taught the bird to mimic human speech, a practice yet popular when Shakespeare wrote Hotspur's line in *Henry IV* , "Nay, I'll have a starling shall be taught to speak...." Starlings have been reported to imitate barking dogs, ringing telephones, revving lawnmowers, and at least fifty-six other bird species from the herring gull to the chestnut-sided warbler. In P.L. Travers's *Mary Poppins,* starlings talk with babies and join them in laughing at the adults who can never understand. According to one account, the birds actually do engage in play, having been observed sledding down snowy roof peaks on their tales. Their talent for organic chemistry has also been noted. Starlings gather the foliage of fleabane and wild carrot for a nest lining that deters blood-sucking fowl mites. How do they locate these herbs? By smell: during breeding season they can scent as acutely as rats. Finally, farmers sensitive to crop destruction should also recognize starlings as the chief predator of the clover weevil, the cutworm, and the Japanese beetle. In the wastelands of surburban lawns they gobble up European crane flies.

Malevolent in flocks, starlings offer the cup of sympathy when seen in single numbers—even dead. I first realized this as a teenage taxidermist. I remember putting aside the block I'd been fashioning for a breast support and fingering my specimen's plumage. It was soft and springy and dappled with tiny, white stars, and among these I found the colors of the rainbow shimmering, as purely radiant as any on earth.

Frogs

Pity the poor frog. You can see a glum fatalism in the look of a captive croaker that vies for eloquence with Sophocles. A frog is a mouse without cunning, a sheep without a shepherd, an erstwhile evolutionary maverick now become everyone's prey. Cars, coons, herons, water snakes, inspired children—all dispatch our few dry-country frogs whenever they get the chance.

A Cascades red-legged frog sulks among whirligig beetles in our kitchen aquarium. Its skin is an exhalant glad-bag; its belly a poached egg. Sleek-headed, the color of pond scum, if it could talk I would expect it to say that there are more predators on heaven and earth than are dreamed of in our philosophy. But to my son's way of thinking, this leggy gherkin pickle is only the same Mr. Jeremy Fisher he has been reading of in his story book. Beatrix Potter's frog eats butterfly sandwiches and grasshoppers in ladybird sauce. Lacking these condiments, I have been tweezering black ants into the bowl, where now they scramble shamelessly across the surface of our unwilling guest. The frog hunkers further into itself, blinking when an ant skittles across its eyeball.

As if to match the frog's long slide to the basement of the food chain, literature records its decline in cultural status. Frogs became princes in German folk tales and agents of godly wrath in the Bible. Northwest tribes revered them as wisdom keepers. Africans made frogs into good-luck necklaces or sacrificed them to bring rain. Medieval Europeans thought they bore clusters of jewels in their heads; they made amphibious potions in defiance of city religion, chanting,

> Fire burn and cauldron bubble.
> Fillet of a fenny snake,
> In the Cauldron boil and bake
> Eye of newt and toe of frog...

By the turn of the century, the frog's close cousin appears as the sanguine Squire Toad, Kenneth Grahame's picaresque hero of *The Wind in the Willows*. Toad experiments with motorcars, gets imprisoned for theft, then fights a great battle with an army of weasels. He overindulges in cigars and celebrates his bad attitude in a ballad.

All of this is to point out that frogs, and nature in general, perhaps, have fallen from the world of symbols. Erstwhile objects of reverence, fear, and trickster comedy, now they are hapless victims. *Natural History* magazine documents the collapse of frog populations worldwide, intimating curtains for the rest of us. The only recent literary frog I can name is the one devoured by a water beetle in Annie Dillard's *Pilgrim at Tinker Creek*.

It's rough out there in the wetlands, but my son and I will return our kitchen frog to his home behind the shed. Then, until the jaws of bass or bullsnake close down on it, our frog can hang at the lid of the pond, spread-eagled like a skydiver. It can mire itself in winter and croon the blues come springtime.

Chimps and Us

The curse of the inspired scientist lies in being misunderstood. Among those with reason to say so are Deborah and Roger Fouts, co-directors of the Chimpanzee and Human Communication Institute at Central Washington University in Ellensburg. Since the late

1960s, the Foutses have pioneered efforts to bridge the species barrier. Their research in teaching American Sign Language to chimps has made them legends in the field of behavioral psychology.

Meanwhile, their colleague of thirty years, an African-born chimp named Washoe, has independently taught the gestural language of the deaf to others of her kind. There are now several chimpanzees at the university who converse in ASL as a native language, both among themselves and with their human associates. These achievements have allowed for breakthroughs in the study of linguistics, which in turn have led to such practical benefits as the teaching of sign language to autistic and brain-damaged humans, persons who had not been able to communicate otherwise. I myself have learned a useful sign from Washoe. It is made by linking together in a chain the thumb and middle finger of each hand, and it means "friend."

Unfortunately, the news that humans are not alone at the pinnacle of life has brought travail to the Foutses. Like Galileo before them, Roger and Deborah have had to weather the suspicion of authorities, among them a university administration that routinely denies funding to the Institute. The Foutses have likewise persisted despite the whims of academic fashion. Rather than learn from the animals who evolved with us, many scientists have scrambled to exclude them from their ever more attenuated definitions of language and intelligence. With the patience of Darwin, the Foutses also have endured the sneers of the ignorant, such as a talk-show host's crack about special ed classes for chimps.

I asked Deborah Fouts, an urgent, blue-eyed woman, why her critics react so scornfully. What blinds them to the evidence that life on earth is of a piece, and that humans are but one kind of animal? "People just don't know where to *put* someone who is so close to us," she said, alluding to the fact that chimps share 98 percent of our genetic material, and are actually closer to us in evolutionary terms than they are to gorillas. Since Aristotle first divided "man" from the animal kingdom, Deborah says, Western scholars have usually sought to defend our status. Only humans made tools, it was once agreed, but then wild chimps were observed fashioning diggers to unearth edible termites. Then again, it was thought, perhaps only we used humor, experienced love, imagined things not physically present. Perhaps only we had language.

One by one, flat-earth hypotheses about human uniqueness have been consigned to cobwebs. On miles of videotape, Washoe and other sign-using apes have documented their rich, oddly familiar mental life. And in doing so, they suggest we listen more closely to ravens, otters, dolphins, and the rest of nature we sometimes consider insensible.

Talking with the Foutses, one realizes how insufficiently their work has been countenanced. As we face a future in which habitat destruction and mass extinctions rapidly occur—a time when one of Washington's senators can glibly state that Northwest salmon would be cheaper to euthanize than to protect—the Chimpanzee and Human Communication Institute is helping to cobble the ark we abandoned long ago. Heeding the prudence of Noah, they make room for our cousins on board.

Namesayers

Early this morning I was out shooing a cow that had no business trampling underfoot a swath of camas in our pasture. She was a sturdy, splay-hipped Angus with a crocodilian talent for oozing under fences where the ground holds water. I was faking to my right, and she was dodging left when a call note suddenly cut the air and arrested the two of us where we stood: "Cur-*lew!* Cur-*lew!*"

said the eponymous long-billed wader, and I guessed it *was* a curlew by that pair of syllables without even sighting the bird, though I knew well enough to look for the profile of arched wings and the curved reed of a bill. The cow broke wind loudly then, and we resumed our chase in spite of the bird's distraction.

But as I was bicycling to work later on, the curlew put me in mind of other name-saying birds, and they in turn released the obvious question: "How do they learn to speak?"

There are the dickcissel, the bobolink, the whippoorwill and the humble chickadee, and who among those raised in a northern forest is not transfixed by the call of the veery? Native in our region to Idaho's panhandle and the eastern uplands of Washington and Oregon, this bird wets the eyes of woods-walkers by a seeming ability to harmonize with itself. Singing "*Vee*-yur, veer-veer-veer" it broods many a green thought in a green shade thanks to the possession of a syrinx, or voice box, that is textured like a reed. Humans can approximate the veery's sound by playing clarinets in duet or by blowing across stalks of summer grass for a humbler effect.

While northern shrikes cannot actually shriek, the Anglo-Saxon name befits this predator of songbirds. Shrikes are sometimes called butcher birds for their habit of impaling prey on barbed wire or thorn tips, whereafter they feed at leisure.

Magpies take their name from vocal behavior, albeit indirectly. According to one source, "magpie" combines "Margaret" with "pika," which means "little girl" in the Scandinavian tongues. Hence the name is said to refer to "a chattering female." Magpies themselves remind most people of rowdy adolescents in gangs—of whatever sex. And if their vocal mimicry has displeased misogynists, well, don't blame the bird. Recent research in neurobiology proves that male birds have larger song-control regions in their brains than females do.

Moreover, it is the male of the avian world that tutors his young in singing. Although mallards and gulls develop their voices innately, songbirds must *learn* their repertoires in a gradual process that may take weeks or months. Experiments have shown that nestlings raised in isolation fail to master song, and that, like humans, birds depend on a "critical age" for language learning. The familiar white-crowned sparrow studies his father's calls between days ten and fifty after hatching. Past that age, a bird will never gain proficiency.

So long as there are birds to call we will be taken by their voices. I can't say the same for cows.

Circling Salmon

Some stories only improve with retelling. Consider that of the anadromous salmon. Sockeye, for example, hatch as needle-sized fry in creek beds throughout the northern Pacific Rim from Japan to California. Baptized in ferocity, they are harried and feasted on by predators. Yet surviving smolts grow and thread their way downstream to nursery lakes, eventually fanning out into the open ocean. There the fish spend three years schooling as lithe, deep-sea swimmers. They mix with stock of far-flung origin, devouring amphipods and squid. At last, one spring, genetic urges call them home again. Using celestial cues and magnetic fields, the fish swim night and day until they find their native river mouth. In brackish estuaries they feed for the last time and then forge upstream past unthinkable obstacles. In their culminating act, sockeyes breed and expire.

To gain the salmon's view of life we would have to spend time underwater. So don your mask and rubber fins with me; let's do our journeywork among the creatures Thoreau described as "animalized water." Imagine we are now below the surface, offshore of British Columbia, where—looking up—we observe silvery sea-runners as an overhead mirage, backlit by the sun and buoyed by green expanses. Hunters—seals and orcas—appear at our periphery in the Strait of Georgia, and seasons later we throng among scarlet homecomers. Later still we drift to the sands of a lake bed where decomposing salmon bodies, vital just hours before, give back their nutrients. But over here we find late-arrivals even now in the act of spawning. Inches above the gravel, riding erect pectorals, the fishes' eyes bulge and their mouths gape strenuously. Dorsals project upright through clouds of milt. This is the moment of supreme resonance. It ends in death.

I've been looking at photographs, as you may have guessed, in particular a portfolio published by the artist Hiromi Naito. The tale they tell has been recounted in literature (Henry Williamson's classic *Salar the Salmon* comes to mind) and in lord knows how many predictable nature films. Naito's collection of stills makes it new. The artist followed sockeye runs for eight years, and during this time he learned more about salmon than their aesthetic qualities. For instance, his are the first pictures I have seen which record the so-called "sneaker male" phenomenon. Sneakers are less powerful breeders who manage to pass their genes on anyway by avoiding sparring contests with alpha males. Darting in among spawning couples at the critical moment, they achieve immortality by virtue of stealth instead of aggression.

Other salmonid facts are more familiar, though they take on charged immediacy in photographs. For example, one of the salmon's navigational tools is its sense of smell. So acute is it that a bear's paw immersed in an upstream pool can halt migration for five minutes. In one experiment, half the cohos running the Issaquah River had their nasal sacs plugged with cotton. Thereafter, at convergences of tributaries, the normal salmon all chose their natal stream correctly, while the nose-plugged fish selected at random.

If conservative politicians succeed in dooming the Northwest's native runs, it won't be the fault of gifted researchers or artists like Hiromi Naito. The failure of imagination, the willful cheapening of character is not theirs.

Surely it is a sign of health when we, too, long to make our life a circle of intimate beginnings, lusty wanderings, and such profound loyalty to place that in our destiny we love and die at home. May the salmon's circle be unbroken.

Wild Encounters

Oreamnos americanus, the mountain goat, is a shaggy, snow-colored beast with stiletto horns that lives about as close to heaven as the surface of our planet will take you. I have been watching a band of these cliff-climbers off and on for five seasons, spotting them through binoculars in a meadow below West Mountain, east of the Cascade Crest. During that time I have heard the bleating of spring kids. I've observed a violent clash between billies. And I've been privileged with the sight of a behavior that goat expert Douglas Chadwick calls "war dancing"— goats leaping straight up into the air, twisting, bucking, tossing their horns, and glissading downhill on hard-packed snow.

All this should have satisfied a casual enthusiast. Yet I'd never come close enough to look one of these animals in the face. Mountain goats are not only extremely agile on inclines that would stop your heart, but they are also wary of primates. Nevertheless, this time out I wanted more than the false intimacy that field glasses afford. I'd been preoccupied with mountain goats since I first found my legs in a range of peaks no wild goat ever climbed. I'd collected a small library of *Oreamnos* literature. Now I was dreaming of goats in my tent at night. I wanted to smell them, walk with them, and hear them speak.

As I lay awake, staring at the nylon ceiling of my shelter, it occurred to me that my obsession must have been common in the past, when animals mattered. Today, wild creatures are vanishing from our mental terrain at a pace that matches their disappearance from the landscape. On the other hand, there are naturalists and probably a few hunters for whom the power of wild encounters remains vivid. No matter how often in a lifetime they meet in close quarters with orcas, wapiti, or courting loons, the intensity of the experience is sharp. "Seeing is believing," we say—and the force of wild things seen attentively can stir the blood.

I was burrowed into my sleeping bag as I thought these thoughts, but sleep would not come. I rolled over, switched on a pen light, and began to page through my anthology of animal poems. In Robert Frost's narrative, "The Most of It," a woodsman echoing his voice off a lakeshore cliff is answered by the visitation of an enormous buck: it "landed pouring like a waterfall, / and stumbled through the rocks with horny tread, / and forced the underbrush—and that was all." Though some people read these lines ironically, as in "*that* was *all?* (we were expecting more)," I found them consoling now, as I meditated on mountain goats. Frost claims no mystical insights unavailable to common readers. He doesn't make of the animal a compensatory self, but he captures the charged physical thrill of its presence.

At daybreak I broke camp and scrambled up a shoulder of the mountain where paintbrush bloomed with clumps of pungent yarrow. Soon I began to notice tufts of fleece decorating the grass. Gaining a saddle, I stepped over piles of droppings. If I faltered here, I would step into thin air. Then we appeared to one another. A great billy goat clambered up and over the cliff's edge just as I rounded a boulder. Our eyes locked; we snorted in shared astonishment; the billy backed over the cliff again—and that was all.

Down Along the Spit

W E'VE COME TO TAKE the sea air. Lori, Erik, and I have driven over mountain passes where snow gathers fir trees into the clouds and semi trucks roar so close at hand we feel our mouths go dry. We have dodged traffic on the coastal plain at the margins of the great city. We've crossed Puget Sound on a ferry boat and downshifted through darkness on rural byways. At Mountain Paul's Taxidermy and Espresso, we sip hot drinks beneath the grimace of a bobcat, then take to the road for the final distance, pulling into our rented cottage as the moon breaks through cumulonimbus clouds. Now, at last, after the car doors click, the cool syllables of breakers reach our ears. Like anyone who travels to the sea, we breathe deliberately.

Dungeness Spit trolls its windy fish hook into the Strait of Juan de Fuca in the rain shadow of Hurricane Ridge and a coil of Olympic peaks. According to the place mats in a local diner, it forms the longest perennial sandbar in North America. We walk the spit at first light, as we will each morning for the half-week we've allotted, and there, like any pilgrims to the sea, we find more than we'd thought to look for. A seashore returns innocence to the landlocked. Among the wrack we can pleasure in crabs and cockle shells and rediscover child's play. But also, a body may look to sea as into dark trees or a snowstorm—then the ocean hints of less intelligible matters.

On our first morning, Lori, Erik, and I seek the surf side of the bar. A strong breeze kicks up whitecaps in the Strait. We meet no one, for in the fogbank that overtakes us there is nobody to meet. Other than the skeletons of pelagic birds, few signs of animal life are present, either. Our heels leave no trace in the sand, washed featureless as it is by every wave cycle's aftermath. Foam curtains scour our tracks from the beach and withdraw in a suck of cobbles. After we imprint our presence again, they curl toward land once more and delete all record of progress. It is the way of a windward coast to practice erasure. Although we are tourists, we walk near breakers to find our proper scale. There is nothing we have to do except put one foot in front of the other and witness shells and smooth stones retreating from our grasp while hard light on water makes the world a photographic negative. A solitary grebe dives beneath the swells offshore. In the manner of all grebes, this one may be taking prey below, but not knowing that you'd think it hunted fruitlessly.

The wind and surf are almost too loud for talk. Instead, they breed remembered voices. I consider the words of King Lear addressing a thunderstorm: "You owe me no subscription....Let fall your horrible pleasure!" Self-mocking now, but half in earnest, too, I let myself hear the poet Gallway Kinnell: "It is written in our hearts, the emptiness is all." Down along the spit, a short walk from well-appointed vacation houses, nature exposes its boneyard. The beach is a record of vanishings.

We hike along as best we can manage, cajoling four-year-old Erik with promises of chocolate nibs and cheese sticks. Drift logs obstruct our passage like a scattering of vast construction toys. Tubes of bull kelp lie coiled on the sand, while several miles distant, Dungeness Light appears to rise from the sea. Lori speaks of the Virginia Woolf novel, *To the Lighthouse*, whose tragedies culminate in a long-postponed excursion offshore. I answer by recalling the epitaph of my great-grandfather, Henry Pennypacker, which is incised in black slate near the Massachusetts beach that Thoreau described as "a wild, rank place" and "a vast morgue." The marker reads: "I hope to see my Pilot face to face when I have crosst the bar." Musing on Tennyson's poem, I have no doubt which side of the bar old Henry expected to face in death, nor why he met chaos with comforting words. I look seaward and squint into wind-whipped spray. To our right, meanwhile, where the spine of the beach rises little more than ten feet above the tide line, the mist appears to thin. Pearly sunbeams appraise the saltgrass there. I turn my head seaward before we climb the dune, wondering what reluctance holds me here. Lori and Erik have already made for the calm, leeward shore. I want to follow, but I want to stay. A longing for two worlds at once is the origin of the backward glance. In my mind I am Orpheus, my wife condemned to Hades by the fickleness of my attention.

At the dune crest, I remember a watercolor from an upstairs bedroom in Grandpa Tom's place, the beach house he inherited from Henry. In my mind's eye, the forms of the painting converge on a woman in a purple dress carrying a handbag. Her back to the viewer, she is climbing up flagstone stairs through a tunnel of vegetation. Down below, the staircase darkens into leaf cover. Beyond, at the scene's upper right corner, it curves out of sight. Sunlight colors the canopy where you imagine them arriving. The walker is poised in the act of raising her right knee to take the weight of another step. There she stands, perennially midway.

Before I cross the spit, I remember another scene. It is the day Lori and I were married ten years ago, and my uncles have ferried our wedding party to the same barrier beach Thoreau visited. Everyone swims on the bayside where the water ebbs warmly over starfish and scuttling hermit crabs. But I am anxious to impress our guests with the open Atlantic, so I persuade a group of friends to ford the dunes. Over on the windward shore, we watch the surf rising in icy, green swells. The beach is vacant. While the rest of us deliberate, my bride sprints headlong into the sea.

Still hesitating on the dune, I watch Lori and Erik shedding their boots and making footprints beside the tracks of a large bird, perhaps a crow or a herring gull. I will rejoin them soon. For the present I have planted my own feet on the verge of some new and (for me) impressive mental territory, and I want to gather what I can there. William James defines epiphany as a two-part process comprising "an uneasiness" and its "solution." The moment of insight that triggers phase two is "a place of conflux where the forces of two universes meet." I watch my son leave the tracking game to chase a great blue heron. He pumps his little arms to mimic the bird's laborious wingbeats. It seems to me, pausing where I can survey both sides of the beach, that Erik unwittingly feels in his limbs what James described—a full participation.

At last I shuffle down the embankment, filling my rubber moccasins with sand. Twenty-five yards make a continent of difference on Dungeness Spit. Walking now in the lee of dunes and driftwood, we watch the bay come alive with movement and significance. Fleets of widgeons and oldsquaws cruise in shallows thick with shrimp. We see goldeneyes, mergansers, scoters, and common loons. Tiny buffleheads, the chickadees of the water fowl, uncork their wee exuberance while Erik rains pebbles over the water. I pick up a stranded jellyfish that spills from my hands like plasma. Yellow sand verbena bloom improbably in the microclimate of a sheltering log. In the words of Darwin, "our most thickly inhabited forests appear almost as deserts" compared to the teeming seashore.

Now Erik rushes a flock of Western sandpipers. Instantly, a scatter of birds probing the tide line for lugworms becomes a mobile constellation. Rising, wheeling, tilting in perfect synchrony, they seem more like a wave pattern than a collection of individuals evading a predator. Chaos theorist James Gleick describes how complex group behavior may arise from simple interactions: in the case of birds, none deliberately leads or abets the patterning. Each one simply sticks close to its neighbors, and each knows how to swerve around obstacles. As a result, we see a collective design invisible to the flock's members themselves. The flight constellation is just a means of not being eaten. Earthbound humans lack the third dimension of birds and schooling fish, but Gleick says that we, too, form predictable patterns. Consider the spectacle of subway patrons navigating a crowded terminal. What beauties might we comprise while avoiding bruised feet? Stressed out and preoccupied as we are, adults yearn for the metavision we attribute to kids and animals. The pull of landscape's edges, its riverbanks, cliffs, and coastlines, is a call to wake up from habit's sensory coma.

The west wind begins to lull as the sun reaches toward noontime and casts a modest November warmth. Fog rolls offshore on the surf side. We walk the estuary beach until I hear my voices return, this time countering the voices to windward. "I thought the earth remembered me," murmurs the poet Mary Oliver, "she took me back so tenderly." And Kinnell again, reaching through some personal abyss, affirms that emptiness "is how we have learned, the embrace is all." Lori and I walk hand in hand, not speaking, but sensing that plenty's horn lies within the contours of our touch.

Back at the cottage, we watch evening slide into pewter seas beyond Port Angeles. The wind has died altogether. We cradle mugs of cocoa, imagining night along the spit and weighing our covenant with wildness and our covenant with ease. At that moment, the picture window frames a final scene ahead of darkness. Perched in a shore pine, a dozen yards from our sitting room, an eagle tears the breast of a mallard hen with its keen, yellow bill.

In a Finch's Beak

WHEN OUR congressman came to town last week, currying favor for voting lockstep 100 percent of the time with Speaker of the House Newt Gingrich, some in the audience could not suppress their enthusiasm. In times like these, dealing pork to weapons producers while venting aggression on the poor is *de rigeur.*

But it seemed to others of us that the congressman's main achievement was his dead-zero score for conservation voting. From the Hanford nuclear clean-up to national park protection, from mining and grazing reform to the Clean Water Act, the congressman had given thumbs down. Not surprisingly then, in his speech to our town-hall audience the man reserved his sharpest barbs for the Endangered Species Act. "I've got nothing against wildlife," he said, but it makes no sense to reign in corporate enterprise when the water is "cleaner than necessary." Businesses are crying for relief, apparently, and besides, he said, "we can't save every species"—it's too expensive. "We've got to bring some balance back to the equation," because "people count, too." After swallowing a few more of these bromides, I felt like a trapped coyote ready to chew its leg off as the price of liberty. But curse the luck, I was seated front and center and in no position to escape. Shifting peevishly in my chair, I wondered what it is about people who say "again" when they are not repeating anything, as in "Again, good science will show us"... ?

What good science shows us is that the number of species on earth is plummeting at a rate 1,000 to 10,000 times higher than in prehuman history. What good sense tells us is that this is being carried forth by the one species able to test, empirically, its dependence on operative ecosystems. Furthermore, the anti-environmental cause is advanced specifically by politicians who ignore recommendations of the National Academy of Sciences.

A thousand miles north of our town hall there lies a vast land of caribou, muskoxen, polar bears, and an array of sea creatures unimaginable in scale. Native people have lived respectfully among them for years, and even today, the only crass intruders are airborne millionaires gunning for wolves. Say hello to the Arctic National Wildlife Refuge. It has several times been targeted for destruction by members of Congress, including our local rep, because there may be fuel reserves beneath its windswept plains. The U.S. Geological Survey estimates the maximum yield as a mere ninety days worth of fuel, but no matter, when it comes to exploiting nature it's not the money, it's the principle of the thing.

Meanwhile, about four thousand miles to the south of our town hall, twenty-five years of field work by the scientists Rosemary and Peter Grant have yielded oceans of data about endangered habitats—and a parable. The parable concerns the cactus finch, one of thirteen species of finches that Charles Darwin studied when he visited the Galapagos Islands in 1835. Besides proving evolution by natural selection once and for all, the Grants have recorded a curious and deadly behavior on the part of this mostly unremarkable bird. Cactus finches depend on their namesake. Without the pollen, the nectar, the fruits, and the seeds of cactus, the birds would go extinct. Yet when they visit a cactus flower, some finches are prone to snipping the stigma, a hollow tube that extends from the center of each blossom. Once its stigma is cut, the flower is sterilized: it wilts without bearing fruit. In normal cactus years, the finches get by. A bad year comes and they starve. The cactus finch may one day cease to exist, a victim of its own meddlesome habits.

Thinking of Galapagos birds or grimacing at a politician's photo-op, I can imagine no dirtier way to treat future generations than to ravage habitat as we are doing. In the exaggerated comfort of our lives, we pretend immunity from natural selection. But as they say, nature bats last. Like cactus finches, many in Congress want to profit the individual at the expense of the flock. Their work is folly, and it should stop.

My Old Arcadia

THE LAST WORKING farm in Glove Hollow, in the mountains of northern New England, overlooked a few dozen acres of cornfield, orchard, and pastured granite where Whetstone Brook tumbles into the Pemigewasset. It was home to a collie named Jack and a family named Huckins, and a more ragtag place you've never seen. The poultry shared such affection you couldn't tell turkey from goose or laying hen, the outbuildings leaned on two-by-fours, and three of seven rollicking kids were fosters from the state—I think they lived on thimbleberries. But Don Huckins was the voice of Glove Hollow. I would meet him crossing his cows to graze, and he would call out to me as I trotted by on running shoes, "I oughta rope you in to do some choahs, you're wastin' your energy!" Jack would grin as only a collie can grin, then he would pace me a stretch before turning to bark the cows along.

On into the seventies, Glove Hollow was a place where kids ran wild. Boys tied squirrel tails to their bicycle handlebars, the owners having gone into the stew pot, while as an annual summer camper there, my own talisman was a salt-cured porcupine paw that hung from a thong around the neck. With a friend named Jay-boy Brown, I dug for antique bottles beneath the mill dam. We hunted fruitlessly for ginseng because it was held to be profitable, though nobody ever divulged a good location so we could find out for ourselves.

Years later, when my wife, Lori, and I had settled down in Glove Hollow, we explored the creek behind Huckins's farm. We were searching for ostrich fern shoots one day, which curl in springtime like violin pegboards and taste like watercress. We hiked through hobblebush and wakerobins until we came out in a high pasture that some Huckins had opened in catamount days. Don Huckins had once kept goats there (before he "swore them off") and they would browse freely with Jack's predecessor, Jack, on watch. It was now a haven for the fox and the partridge. Huckins called it Skyfields. A scatter of trailer homes clung to the edge of a drumlin there, each taking in prospects of four counties without a weekend house in sight. At twilight, we turned cartwheels through waist-high grass in view of Moose Hillock and the Ossippee Range. We found the gnarled oak whose branches made a room, then pulled ourselves closer to the evening star.

Glove Hollow was a good, green world. But then one year my job at the community college ended, and Lori had begun to polish her dissertation. So we put New England behind us and followed the beck of opportunity where it would lead. From New Hampshire to South Carolina, one teaching contract succeeded another. Glove Hollow remained behind us, a clearing in the forest we always meant to circle back to. These days, however, one of us is finally traveling the tenure track, and we have taken root in central Washington. Between the east slope of the Cascade Mountains and the Columbia Basin there lies an egg-shaped valley of cattle ranches and wheat farms. Broad prairies that top out in sagebrush drain evenly toward the Yakima River and the college-and-rodeo town of Ellensburg. Beyond the sagebrush are ponderosa foothills to the north and west. To the south and east we can walk among canyons, lupine-fretted steppes, and cactus domes. The volcanoes, Rainier and Adams, are visible here, and residents on the west side of the river take in vistas of the Stuart Range. In its natural state, the Kittitas Valley is a land of ecotones. An afternoon's hiking may carry you through belts of semi-desert inhabited by bighorn sheep, alluvial channels where beavers work to the calling of Western tanagers, and dense fir groves concealing the cougar's track. Here is the country of the eagle. Here we find ravens.

Above all, though, we are aware of living in a land of manifest destiny. Down in the valley, you couldn't blaze a curved, irregular path if you shortened one of your legs. Streets and county roads comprise an undeviating gridwork, and—more so even than the doublewides that house the populace—fences are this country's architectural emblem. Seven strands of tightly stretched barbed wire brook no human passage, I have found. One looks in vain for the stiles that breached Don Huckins' fences. Our local totem is the beef cow, whose grazing must be managed, but make no mistake about survey lines. They are here to assert dominion. Robert Frost, the bard of New England, wrote a poem on this subject that is remembered mainly for the line reading, "Good fences make good neighbors." In context, the words are understood ironically, but in our valley the mention of neighbors would be thought merely irrelevant. The local formulation might be stated, "Good fences make good property." (Now keep moving, stranger.)

Enter the woods and highlands above the Kittitas, and if you had the senses of a Northeast neophyte, you might be tempted to suppose them a last wild paradise. So much unpeopled land extending beyond the horizon! Stick around, though, and feel the earth shudder with the passage of ORV riders on all those miles of logging road you'd thought were fine for hiking. Thread your way through a streamside canopy to discover clearcuts the size of New England townships. When the dust settles and the roaring fades, consider the song of the varied thrush: twin-noted, dirge-like, it might be a requiem for abandoned sympathies.

One morning in spring a few years ago, homesick for birches and maple trees, my wife and son and I took a walk at sunrise. We had to get in our car to do it since towns and "open space" are separate worlds in the West. But at last we set out in a state park that hugs the Yakima River shoreline. We arrived in high mating season. Hermit thrushes, Audubon's warblers, and lazuli buntings conducted their sonic courtships from aspen bough to cottonwood limb the length of our trail. Nootka roses leafed in yellow light. At one point we heard a flock of Canada geese blaring full-throatedly, then watched the familiar "V" appear, its angle pointed east. A decision seemed to accomplish itself. Shouldn't we follow the geese? Take that summer job we'd been offered in Vermont? Learn, like birds, to live bi-regionally? Back at the house we made our calls, shoed the mules, and followed the interstate flyway back to New England.

Imagination is a tease according to the poet John Keats, especially when it romances nature. Or maybe we live in a disjointed time. At any rate, you can leave your home behind for seven years, then return and tally the losses. If your list comes out shorter than mine, you might want to conceal your address.

We dropped our car in Laconia and took an afternoon creek hike to clear from hindsight the billboards along I-93, the new condos on Black Mountain, and the hayfields converted to pavement. Poised to leap from stone to stone, I thought of a time when beauty was unremarkable. Though we'd crossed no fences, it occurred to me that even this modest creek must now be someone's prized possession. Did northern New England still exist, I wondered? My life had circled back this way so often since the days I tagged along to the Browns' summer place, a sprout in Cub Scout blues. But the reach of the land's appeal must have tipped off Jay-boy's parents about predations to come. They sold their farmhouse in 1970 and bought another in Nova Scotia.

Back then, the hillsides still made grass for dairies, and bottom acres grew field corn. Lonesome wilds of moose and fir seemed impenetrable north of St. Johnsbury. South were the Appalachian Trail, funky river towns like Bellows Falls (Fellow's Balls to rival high school teams), and naturally there were countless pure and steepled whistle stops, visible testimony to John Dewey's ideal of democracy: Surrey, Sandwich, Washington, and Lyme, Newfane, Danville, and Craftsbury. Tourist traps and throbbing ski tows were exceptional and welcome to my child's eyes. Though exotic Hassidim had summered in Bethlehem for years, Mr. Brown thought the northland sufficiently remote from the building booms of southern New England. "It's just too-oo far to drive," he said, until he surprised everyone and abruptly sold. Now the interstate bisects Franconia Notch, and if old Robert Frost had lived to look on from his porch at Sugar Hill, poems like "Design" might have sought their imagery among the "assorted characters" of earth removal.

Momentum is the secret of creek hiking. The afternoon of our return, we found that if we trusted a rock to meet our next leap it generally did, and we kept our feet more dry than wet by simply going forward, not pausing to deliberate. But this practice makes a poor analogy for community planning. Resorting to the gallows humor common among upland Yankees, a friend had written, "The land's been raped, 'development' is a pregnant word, and *Roe v. Wade* is in eclipse." From across the river that borders New Hampshire and Vermont, another friend had sent word of his town's yuppie transformation. Responding in kind, I asked about a nearby ski resort. Would his creek run dry if they drained the watershed for snowmaking? My family had returned seeking refuge from conflict but found the day too late, our creek hike overshadowed by hemlocks and regret. At the shore of that bought-and-paid for brook, underneath the maples, an ovenbird said, "*Dee*-per."

Conflict, I remembered, can seem to dictate relationships in the West. Few Westerners stay put long enough to learn to get along. As among people anywhere, the good, the indifferent, and the sinister are found in equal measure East and West, the difference being that westward, the sinister are better armed. At first I embraced the Kittitas for its lack of class divisions. Then came the day during hunting season when I trespassed on someone's outback, and I found myself hugging a tree while the bullets flew.

The summer's job, like any academic term, transpired in a blur. We collected ourselves for an earnest self-assessment. What prospects would bring us East again? As it happened, our migration turned where it had begun years before, at the house of a neighbor in Glove Hollow. From the loft of her barn, where we retrieved half-forgotten furniture, I could look down the road to the steep-roofed rectangle that had once been our home. Since the nineteenth century, two public buildings have defined the hamlet as a place. One is the falling-down grange where old timers serve red-flannel hash, and the other, Glove Hollow Schoolhouse, which Lori and I had rented. Don Huckins learned to read in our bedroom/living room/kitchen ("for all the good it did him," as Lori testily observed one day at town meeting, when Huckins orated some piece of sarcasm from *The Manchester Union Leader*). The stove we heated with released much of its smoke through a pipe to the outdoors. The rest we were willing to cope with for the sake of a back porch we could sit on during eight weeks of the year and a view through poplars to meadow land beyond. After the meadow came woods threaded with trails, and after the woods, the Skyfields hill. Our rental pickup loaded to go, we walked the land again in the spirit you bring to nostalgic occasions. Each step felt tentative, as though the ground were softer than late summer rains would warrant. We avoided Skyfields and the Huckins's place, too. Instead we drove over to Waterton Valley and looked in on a friend.

Nat Holmquist, son of Peace Corps doctors who kept a farm in Waterton, had always meant to show us where he gathers chanterelle mushrooms on the trail to Painted Cliff. As chair of the Waterton Valley Athletic and Improvement Association (so named a hundred years ago), Nat has blazed, maintained, or carved signs for most of the local trails that the Appalachian Mountain Club has never heard of. Yet he, his wife Ginny, and the dozen others who comprise the Association, have neglected to post a sign at the head of Painted Cliff Trail. They have let alders overgrow the point of entry. Nat tells of a mountain lion he is certain lives at Painted Cliff, attributing the cat's survival to its art of subterfuge.

That afternoon we found Nat outside his cabin, digging among potato hills. His tall, denim-sleeved figure looked Currier and Ives; you might expect him to leave his plow and march on Virginia for the Union. But now as he turned in greeting, the sunlight showed us his freckles, benign blue eyes, and slow smile, remarkable in a man who walks like a mountain. Nat Holmquist doesn't care if you see the holes in his socks. He is one who makes sense of things, publishing articles on natural history and computer instruction for kids. Yet his way appears leisurely; he is pleased to rest his spade for company, to go for a hike up Kinsman, say, to talk of what he's thought about all winter, and about the misdeeds of the Waterton Corporation.

The town of Waterton was established in the 1760s in much the same way as any New England settlement. Homesteaders cleared the slopes above Mad River for sheep pasture, surveyed a common, and built clapboard houses around it. That is what Nat Holmquist's ancestor found when he arrived a century later. The Holmquist patriarch erected a stone tower in which he founded the first town library, shelving books around a circular staircase and building a reading room at the top. From the tower's summit you can gaze at Mt. Tripyramid, but the common that once lay below has been replaced by tennis courts. Not to worry, advised Bob Conkley, the Waterton Corporation's president. The town green could simply be relocated at the eastern end of his newly planned "recreation facility" for consumers of the slopes and golf links. (And there you may find it now, behind the Loon Saloon and a chocolate fudge shoppe.) Several old houses around the common were purchased also, after which they, too, were carted off or destroyed. Waterton's tale is familiar. The locals play the part of rubes, bought off piecemeal by carefully legal means. The Forest Service had a hand in their duping as well, having leased surrounding mountains to Conkley with the understanding—at least, so it was understood twenty-five years ago—that his terms allowed for "a family ski area of modest proportions."

Well, Modesty is shamed wherever she travels nowadays. Trust New England, wrote Frost in the twenties, "not to have enough of anything to sell." The cruelty of Frost's misjudgment is not lost on Nat Holmquist, nor does it stop him from leading a patient campaign to limit Conkley's theft of more national forest land—public land—in order to groom it and charge trail fees where now you can ski gratis. The afternoon of our visit, Nat led us on a walk to Greeley Pond. We cut across the country-club accommodations that crowd the narrow valley, skirted the margins of a time-share ghetto, and entered the woods where I had once seen a bear. Black bears find bonanzas among the weekenders' trash, Nat said. As we entered the canopy, he told us how difficult it had become to criticize the Waterton Corporation since Conkley bought the local newspaper. But soon we were deeper in the woods and higher up, and if it had been winter, we might have escaped the skilifts' drone.

Now that Lori and I live our lives out West, we fight against homesickness by taking in the sky. From our kitchen window we admire a sweep of it unimaginable in New England. Close up, we find less "biomass" in our adopted country, but we learn to be connoisseurs of sunset and cloud. For their part, transplanted Westerners speak of the horizon sickness they suffer in New England; to compensate, they foster ties with trees. Such ambitions come easily in Glove Hollow, where wildness advances over meadows as in the time-lapse succession of old nature films, grass giving way to steeplebush and pine, hardwood groves overcoming evergreens, forests growing from scratch in a couple of decades.

Out West, the wildness most people experience is a view. We thrill to the sight of our tawny, Kittitas hills, accessible by a fifteen-minute car ride. In the clear air, I can watch my closest neighbors brush their teeth a hundred yards away. East of my house, a farmer raises fine timothy hay with stern doses of poison, and cattle graze the slough below us, trampling the banks of Cattail Creek into an earthen gruel. Further improving views, developers chain-drag the prairie to remove unsightly growth, which happens to be the same bitterbrush and sage I buy from a mail-order nursery in Tekoa.

Back in Glove Hollow, though, I used to find coyote scats on my doorstep. Pileated woodpeckers nested in the cavity of a giant sugar maple that screened our neighbor's house from view. We lived a mile from town by road, a mile and half by footpath through the woods. New England sips nature from a teacup.

In the West we ride, but walking was always our way in the land I called my Arcadia. I remember the day in late November we hiked seven miles into the Pemigewasset Wilderness. It was a brisk morning, about twenty degrees with an inch of snow, but we slipped on icy cobbles while crossing the river and had to run the whole way back for fear of frostbite. On the summit of Osceola the summer before, Nat had read to us from the Book of the Hopi while a thunderstorm lashed our tent stays. The next day dawned so fresh we had climbed up Whiteface Peak by noon. During the last winter that Lori and I lived in Glove Hollow, Nat and Ginny and the two of us took the route to Painted Cliff on skis. December twenty-first it was, and all agreed as we glided away and herringboned up that the coming year would follow under one condition: we had to reach the base of the cliff before it darkened in shadow. With the year's old sun glazing the ice on that south face, we arrived in time to save the world. Then we turned and looked down valley together, where the white mound of Skyfields showed through the falling dusk. I thought I saw blue and orange Christmas lights blinking at Huckins's farm. The sun would not be swallowed up in night. And yet, when I try to recover Glove Hollow, truth has a way of puncturing my fond, bucolic bubbles. The country of home does not exist anymore. It was a good, green world and certain to change, but its changes have killed more than a rural folklife, a dream of integrity. Among the outlet stores and luxury second homes for which the mystery groves of childhood have been leveled, the lakes and maples are dying from acid rain. Exhaust fumes cloud the ski commuter routes. Hillsides are blasted where the heedless will play, and songbirds fail to reappear in spring. Here is my elegy for Glove Hollow, which could be your place or anybody's, though it happens to be mine and I have lost it. It will not be mourned by milkers of the golden calf or missed by anyone but those for whom it was alive.

We are settled now in the Kittitas, where we interpret conflicting signs. There's not a white resident here who can count more than five generations, and development pressure is fierce. The chamber of commerce speaks out against zoning and public transportation. And though winter air inversions are chronic, our newspaper decries a study by the Department of Ecology, predicting "onerous regulations" to follow. On the other hand, residents have helped defeat a statewide property-rights initiative, and locally, our city will soon begin work on a walking trail to connect the downtown with a riverside park. I can't deny that we live in a good place. We've got a freezer full of huckleberries. Jars of dried morels line the pantry. We hike and ski in the Wenatchee Mountains. The soil yields excellent garlic, and we scatter feed for the quail my son stalks with suction-cup arrows. The Kittitas is as good a place as a belated immigrant could hope for. But I can claim no memories here.

Whenever I remember Glove Hollow, it wears the drowsiness of late October. Huckins's farm is quiet: Jack dozing on the porch, the old man woolgathering in his shop. Kids grown and gone, corn all in, snowplow nosed to the front of the barn, a blonde fox sauntering into the trees. Suspended from a yardarm is the shape of a buck, and strange birds color the walkway, pecking at gravel. I like to picture it like this—a few last marigolds around the flag-pole—but I don't know, really, what is there anymore.

Part II

Gaia

THE HUNTER'S MOON climbed a latticework of willows last night. From where we sat in the pasture, eating corn chips, my son said, "The moon doesn't have a face, does it?" I explained that in picture books, many things are made to look like people so kids will know they matter, the moon in Erik's poetry book being a case in point.

"Anyway," I said, trying not to sound pedantic, "the moon has craters that look like eyes, a nose, and a mouth. Do you see them?" Lori recalled how the earth had appeared to her when recorded by moon-bound astronauts—a marbled sphere much more wonderful than the classroom globes of our youth, with their lame color schemes and arbitrary political boundaries.

"But the moon is *real*," Erik insisted. "It's not a person." Then, without skipping a beat, he asked, "Is Mother Earth a person?"

I don't know where he picked up the term, "Mother Earth," and I have no objection to the metaphor as such. But in listening to my son, I found myself reflecting (with far less radiance than the moon reflects) on what may be my own imaginative failure, or on the other hand, the waxing of a trendy cliché. Is nature actually in some sense female, and the planet earth a goddess? Does it matter whether we say so?

Not long after the astronauts brought back their pictures, biologist James Lovelock proposed the Gaia hypothesis. His theory holds that the earth is a single, complex organism, able to regulate its biochemical processes for the purpose of encouraging life. In place of the Enlightenment idea of earth as a machine in a clockwork universe, believers in the new model could perceive it the way our ancestors had, as the body of life—or even a conscious being. To the minds of many, the planet has since been reborn as "Gaia," a name borrowed from the Greek goddess of the earth. Research seems to be upholding Lovelock's idea, at least the scientific part. So far, atmospheric studies and microbiological data alike testify that earth behaves more as a dynamic, physiological system than a static theater for the laws of physics. Therefore, if research trends continue, we can look forward to new ways of thinking on account of what scholars call a paradigm shift.

Many would argue that new ways of thinking and behaving are what's needed in an age of grand-scale extinctions, habitat destruction, and atmospheric poisoning. If addressing the earth in prayer will help to buck these trends, then what is there to object to? When we recognize a thing as sacred we grant it allowances, as on occasion, wartime bombers have spared cathedrals.

My only gripe about Gaia is this: aside from certain specific features, I can't bring myself to recognize nature as a woman. That's not to say I embrace the Old Testament grouch or some other male imago. The oceans, the continents, and the heavens deserve our reverence for all their beauty and danger, but to me, they just don't signify in gender. Lynn Margulis, a colleague of Lovelock's, says admiringly, "Gaia is a tough bitch." Yet no one thinks of Apollo when the sun shines, and the fact that Poseidon was male has always seemed incongruous given the menstrual association of tides. The scholar Susan Griffin argues that feminist metaphors will activate the environmental movement. But do we really need to sex-type nature? Calling the earth our Mother leaves men in the same position as women expected to worship God the Father. Too often, scientific theories are warped for exclusionary purposes when they gain mass approval, the most disastrous case being that of the misnamed "social Darwinism." Gaia worshippers may do comparatively little harm, yet in flirting with affectation, they trivialize a genuine spiritual hunger. As one critic quipped, "My mother's name is Evelyn, not Gaia."

Divinity needs no gender. After all, nature may not require the symbol-worshipping animals who attribute such qualities. "Gaia," says Margulis in a more sober moment, "is Darwin's natural selector." As the sum of all organic interactions, Gaia curbs the growth of any single species when it comes at the expense of others. Indeed, say theorists, the earth is capable of exerting vast counterpressures on human life. You see where my argument is leading. Plagues, famines, climate change—no moral need apply to the earth's corrections, whatever form they take. Populations of bacteria crash all the time, as do famously self-destructive lemmings. Still, we are moralizing animals; we can't help interpreting our fate. We run into problems only because we turn mental conceits into idols and persecute those who refuse them. Now, in homage to the gods of "free" enterprise, we stalk the earth like grave robbers on the way to anatomy class. If Las Vegas bookies figured odds on Gaian survival, our species might go begging for backers.

Fortunately, there is more to the human story. Notwithstanding our flair for violence, our ego saturation, and other unlovely qualities, the best of us also make music and do advanced math. We build chairs, tell jokes. Word games, narratives, and soccer are small but telling items in our behavioral catalogue. Whether creativity can save us in the long run is an open question. But among the inhabitants of Gaia, we know that we were born to wonder. Who's to say? Perhaps by watching a hunter's moon whiten the rounded plain of the earth, my wife, my son, and I were fulfilling our genetic destiny. So we did.

Manastash Ridge

Looking upward from the nadir of the Kittitas Valley, it is possible to imagine Manastash Ridge strutted with chairlifts. Our town's closest highland is uncommonly steep. If profiteers ever have their way with it, I might be able to leave my car in a former hayfield, ride a gondola to the summit, and then peer down at recreation vehicles parked in rows. "Look, there's ours! Let's get a picture of the view." As matters stand, however, I travel Manastash Ridge on foot, another good-timing atavist.

Walking with me today, my friend Sam Clooney remarks on the felicity of these hills. Sam lives back in Vermont, where he studies loons, bagpipes, and stone-age calendar sites. The stern crags of the Stuart Range, visible to the north, are the kind that make him nervous, he says. Taking Sam's thought another way, I allow that Manastash summons female images when I look along its length. I risk offending persons of gender and committing anthropomorphism as well. But, even against my better judgment, I like finding form in that curving knoll, that lap of evergreen.

Somehow, Sam and I have missed the trailhead proper. We follow a spur as best we can, erosion and frozen snow confounding our best intentions until we strap on sets of instep crampons. Even so, the going proceeds by inches. The need for breath replaces conversation until we gain the first shoulder of higher land, at which point we pause to inspect a campfire midden. Some buccaneer has kindled his flame with plastic soda bottles. If we let them lie, we could return in four hundred years and find them unchanged. The need for back-country rules, like "pack-it-in/ pack-it-out," reminds me that escape is a real estate fantasy. There's no dodging our problems out in the bush. It's just quieter.

From now on the summit can be seen from our path. Game trails thread the hillside like veins in a mound of fish roe. Silence muffles the afternoon with cloud cover. Birds are absent, and gray stalks of brush bear witness to energies drawn underground. Even the springtails that graze midwinter snow cannot be found in the weeks before Solstice. Without the company of my friend, I would think I kept an unpopulated world.

At 2,500 feet more company announces itself, albeit in absentia. Tracks begin to criss-cross the trail, first the valentine spoor of deer, then the larger prints of wapiti, also known by the misborrowing of elk from *elg*, the Norwegian word for moose. And here's a coyote. Pedaling by on some errand, it has marked the path with a fur-studded cairn. Evidence of good feed bodes well for winter mating.

Sam looks westward, as deep-set in the eyes as an albatross. Prior to writing a book on the Celtic saint, Columba, Sam traced his hero's route across the Irish Sea in a *carragh*, which is an oval dinghy of hide or canvas stretched over rowan wood. My forbears sailed the same waters in longboats, but I prefer this gusty steppe. When dark November roosts like a greasy cowbird, the lion-colored hills console me.

Entering a pine grove, we hear chickadees sassing the wind. You can jack the temperature down to zero and pelt the Manastash with ice. Bad weather seems only to lift the spirits of this tribe. Chickadees tell of forbearance, like my friend's Irish monk. Sam narrates Columba's flight from Vatican soldiers in the sixth century. It seems the Irish church retained too much nature-love, too little awe for distant authority. With a handful of fellow heretics, Columba fled Ireland and Rome's decree, sailing up the Scottish coast to Iona. From that spare biography has come a welter of legends and folksongs. Sam and I consider how the patron saint of homesickness would feel about the Kittitas Valley. It spreads in patterns of field, grove, and settlement below us, the sort of land an exile might yearn for.

The steel box we find at the summit contains a notebook for hikers. I smooth back its pages and read aloud. Lines of Japanese characters precede an eloquent translation: "I seem to be walking through a painting." A woman confesses romantic sorrow, then gives thanks for the power of open air. Other writers greet absent friends, praise Jesus, or testify for self-esteem. A few record animal sightings and weather data. All, it seems to me, try to eke some goodness out of their day on the ridge. In that effort we come together. Here at the end of a brutal century, what higher calling is there than to heed a chosen landscape?

Our view from Manastash would slake an epic appetite. Cascade horns cut the sky; hills run in waves. The next step for Sam and me is the one that leads down. Back where our lives go on, we've promised to remember what we see.

City Walk

MORNING KINDLED slowly. Weirs of aspen sifted the fog that shrouded Ellensburg. I was out before sunrise by half an hour maybe—who could tell?—but the lean fox catches more rabbits. I wanted to find a city walk.

My second grade teacher had once read from H.C. Holling's *Paddle-to-the-Sea,* which is the name given to a toy canoeist by the Chippewa boy who carves him. He launches the canoe and rider in a Lake Superior tributary, and from there it travels throughout the Great Lakes clear to the Gulf of Saint Lawrence and the open Atlantic. The idea of the book still tickled me. In a town of many watercourses, why not walk the way they flowed, vagabond through school yard and neighborhood, then arrive to see them spill into the Yakima River?

I began my tour where an irrigation ditch elbows the grounds of Central Washington University. "The Ganges" they call it, and like some healing ablution, this canal draws all quarters of the campus. I paused to look from a bridge at street side. Mallards dipped in the shallows, jostling each other as they billed my cracker crumbs. Overhead, a sound like chopsticks meeting revealed a flock of grosbeaks clipping wing-shaped fruits—samaras—from a box elder. Groundskeepers shave these stream banks right to the water's edge. Left to themselves, they'd make a proper setting for the plunge of Hamlet's girlfriend. I saw remnant rushes overhung with willow trees, and aptly enough, the Language and Literature building on my left. Doubtless, somebody would be talking up Shakespeare this morning.

I crossed the next bridge to the Ganges' south shore, then detoured for a look at "Cascade Cradle," the university's sculptural equivalent of a dolmen or the site of a sun cult. Resembling half the shell of a Gemini space capsule balanced on a cone, the piece may speak to functional art enthusiasts and sky worshippers alike. On blustery days, the top section turns with the wind. It channeled down from the mountains today, and so, like Paddle-to-the-Sea, I followed wind and water on an irregular, southwesterly azimuth.

Passing beneath the portals of a Japanese garden, I gazed over bonsai shrubbery, artificial brooks, granite lanterns, and a parallelogram of carefully raked sand meant to demonstrate cosmic mind. The place is exquisite but puzzling. In Cascade Cradle I had seen an artwork dancing with nature; here the theme was improvement. I tried to banish the thought that such a garden does to its plants what hydro-dams do to rivers. Inviting it was, in any case. Idling on a cedar bench for a moment, I could appreciate the gardeners for cultivating rest at the heart of a busy campus. But when I exited by way of a second ornamental gateway, I remembered an early episode in *Paddle-to-the-Sea* when flood waters breach a beaver dam, and the toy canoe escapes, resuming its journey downstream.

Now I found the Ganges path again. I wandered east across Chestnut Mall and out behind a student dorm just now coming to life. Here, against all conceivable hydro-logic, the canal turned wild. Its current sought the twists and oxbows that wend through natural streams. Its banks wore sedges and horsetails. I stole up near a ruddering muskrat. Besides their small stature, these creatures part from their beaver relatives in the working of their tails—side to side like a fish instead of up and down in porpoise fashion. This little friend looked complacent with its mouth full of forage, but I knew that muskrats catch hell from minks and men with survey stakes. How long can any wetland animal escape the onslaught of our population?

Had I launched a toy boat at the first bridge I came to and followed its course, our ways must now have parted at Alder Street. I bid farewell to the Ganges where a culvert took its water underground. The route from this point needed improvising. I wandered cross-lots like an errant paper boy, listening all the while for the liquid sounds that seem to distill a snowless winter. Traffic overlaid its own drones and wheezes. I caught a light at Eighth Avenue and headed for the county fairground. In luck again, I soon smelled an odor like damp tea leaves. A creek lapped forth from still-green weeds, scuddered under the road, then disappeared from view behind a duplex.

I grumble about property when it blocks my path. But privacy I respect. There's nothing to do in a case like this except keep to the public way and watch your quarry from the corner of one eye. In chapter twelve of Holling's book, fishermen rescue Paddle-to-the-Sea from their nets. One man proposes taking the toy home to his nephew. But Paddle slips from his fingers into the lake and is carried away by the waves once again. Canvassing an American town on an errand such as mine, one feels like the fisherman and the journeymaker at once: you want to embrace everything as your own, but then again, you would like to walk away from it all. Two blocks down on Walnut Street I found the creek again, or perhaps some other creek, and a dozen yards beyond I saw the pavement swallow it. I waited while commuters backed their cars onto the street; others appeared on their doorsteps, full of breakfast and purposeful looks. Across the road a school bus was taking on children. I flattered myself that if I could, I would pied-piper those kids to the riverside.

Gordie, an ebullient man in coveralls and a salt-and-pepper butch-cut, hailed me from a block away. Though he would have been called "retarded" in a less sensitive time, Gordie keeps our streets free of aluminum cans, and more importantly, he is the town crier. Every day he travels back and forth from the recycling center, hauling wagonloads of cargo tractor-trailer style behind his bicycle, and any breed of weather finds him as sanguine as another. Gordie is a man of lungs and hyperbole.

"Just got back from deer huntin'—bagged myself an eight-pointer!" he shouted to me now. "Shoulda' seen all the cans there in the parking lot, too—I'm gonna' make five-hundred bucks! Well, I got rid of all that junk in my garage. Them old radio parts must have weighed a ton. Sold it all and bought my niece a coloring book for her birthday. Oh, I feel like an old man with his head caved in!"

Monologic speech asks no rejoinder. But this morning I was happy to be waylaid. After all, even Paddle-to-the-Sea took the occasional hiatus, once wintering out with a prolix Quebecker. Usually when I see Gordie coming, I batten my hatches for a long blow. What would happen if I squeezed a word in edgewise?

"Got a full wagonload," he hollers. "Shoulda' seen the party they had out at Ericksen's!"

"My sister's a trained nurse," I answer. "Works nights at the hospital."

"The Mariners are playin' two games tomorrow!"

"Do you take that with garlic?"

"Gonna eat twelve pizzas. Gotta' keep my strength up!"

"Well, better wash my car before it rains."

"Must be fifty degrees out! Almost knocked my wagon over coming up that hill! Bill Fairchild gave me a new bicycle! Broke my old one in twenty pieces!"

Drowning me out with a final, non-sequitorial rally, Gordie tooled along his way. Meanwhile, the pale, December sun that had escaped my notice in rising retreated again as I stepped into the shadow of Craig's Hill. As Ellensburg's geographical benchmark, the hill was a beckoning hard to resist. I left my creek route temporarily to climb switchbacks among the city's last vestiges of native vegetation. Johnson Meninick of the Yakama nation had told me how the hilltop served as the site for generations of ceremonies. In legend, it signaled to returning salmon that their spawning streams lay just ahead. And it was there at the base of the hill that Yakama villagers lived in numbers exceeding their white neighbors until the turn of the twentieth century.

Recent decades tell a different story. A fortress-like American Legion post occupies the summit beside a parking lot that offers cheap seats during rodeo season. (I peered through links of cyclone fencing at the stadium below.) The city water tower, toothpaste green and blunt as a chamber pot, crests the eastward rim beyond a park of turf and shade trees, and clusters of swank houses overlook the southern slope. I suppose Craig's Hill offers about as much land-use compromise as can be expected in a Western town. But in spite of the public trail I climbed to get here, despite the free parking and the public lawn, people show a meager affection for the earth. The rabbit sage, bitterbrush, balsamroots, and lupines locally extinct elsewhere within city limits have clung to tenuous rootholds on the hill's two or three undeveloped acres. Yet gullies and random bike paths are carved among them. At present, I watched a teenager descending in a mountaineer's glissade while a shower of earth and stones fell around him. The Legionnaires, I'm told, have planned to adorn one stretch of the summit with flag poles.

I rejoined Wilson Creek below the last block of houses and a shade to the east of Canyon Road's franchise strip. Excepting the fast-food trash blowing in here, I walked the most serene stretch of water I'd met with. Densely growing willows broke now and then upon fields of winter wheat. A vacant oriole nest hung from a branch as if in mimicry of the hornet's nest that drooped above it. Perhaps a far cry from the eyries of a Canadian wilderness, these tokens uplifted me anyway. I could smell the Yakima River. My creek veered westward into a culvert now, so I waited for the traffic to wane before crossing the road. Meanwhile, I considered the many delays and obstacles that Paddle-to-the-Sea got past, including Windsor Lock, Niagara Falls, and a stint on a raft of drift logs.

On the far side of the road, cottonwood trees closed ranks around me. I paced along, navigating hardwood bottomlands that some call the Magic Forest. It is here that truants and homeless men repair. I knew that a public fishing area lay somewhere nearby, obscured by understory shrubs. A Volkswagon decayed among Oregon grape bushes; the ground was still russet with fallen hawthorn leaves. In the Magic Forest, you begin to stray from your purposes, if you have any, even one as eccentric as mine. Trees began calling to mind other trees I'd known. In the texture of their trunks I reviewed the morning faces I'd observed back in town. Some were vacant, others fretful or inviting, but each had called for sympathy. "Stranger," Walt Whitman said, "if you passing meet me and desire to speak to me, why should you not speak to me? And why should I not speak to you?" For answer, I found myself listening to the river.

Yet it was a man that spoke up next. A former college professor down on his luck, the clay-colored figure that materialized from a thicket told me he was walking between Eugene, Oregon, and Moscow, Idaho, and that he did so annually. Like Matthew Arnold's scholar gypsy, this man liked to haunt the outskirts of college towns. "I'm alleged to be a danger to myself and others," he warned, but walking was obviously his passion. As proof, he set down his plastic satchel and thrust at me a handful of small stones. These gave geological evidence of the corridor he roamed. Interpreting my silence as doubt, the traveler ordered me to choose from his collection. He stepped closer and peered through a limp wing of hair. "Take the right piece, the one that was meant for you alone," he said. When I pointed to a shard of quartz, the man's posture relaxed. He placed the stone in my hand and folded the fingers over it.

Within minutes I stood by the riverside and craned my neck to see into the mouth of Yakima Canyon. I felt free to imagine Wapato, Hanford Reach, the Columbia Gorge, and the wide Pacific beyond. Before circling for home I cast my quartz pebble to the current, trusting that in time, wave erosion would ferry it grain by grain to the saltwater tides. Like the launching of toy canoes, walking makes sport from humble means. Even Paddle-to-the-Sea returned to its origin at last. The story would carry me back as I had come.

Whiskey Dick

THE NAME prepared us for a getaway where pool sharks and drugstore cowboys might repair. Instead we found ravens, rare spines, and a grizzly token.

Whiskey Dick Mountain rises west of the Columbia River. My family visited on the solstice, a day when winter leapfrogged into the Basin. Fog had shut off the hills that morning, and the air felt neither harsh nor temperate when we pulled off the Old Vantage Highway and into Quilomene Wildlife Recreation Area. I took Erik by the hand while Lori looked around forlornly. All week long I had promised desert air and views to stretch the eye. Now, dense clouds nudged the skeptic in us. Between bites of apple I toyed with the phrase, "wildlife recreation area." Without our sanction, how could the deer and the antelope play? Then we saw a thing I wish we hadn't. From a signpost hung a hamstrung jackrabbit someone had used for shooting practice. My wife and I exchanged head shakes, and I cut free the animal's remains. "Let's get on with it," I said.

A jeep track led us up and down, east and west, and finally to the north, slicing as it did through thickets of sage and greasewood. These shrubs wear the character of any dryland plant. They're sticky, sharp, deeply rooted, and prudent. Desert shrubs obey a stern code. I have driven past so-called desert landscaping in Arizona suburbs, where flora like these mix queerly with the opulent lifestyles common thereabouts. Here, too, in the treeless hills of central Washington, these plants can hinder belonging. We warmed ourselves with conversation as we walked. Yet affinities with other lives, I knew, wanted more than an afternoon to find.

After a mile, the trail switchbacked into a swale. Here stood chest-high stalks of native grass, dried and clicking in the wind. Forebears of these remnants once tickled the ears of Indian ponies. Then came the livestock of the pioneers, and knottier growth spread in their wake. During recent decades, knapweeds and thistles have completed the modern range succession. Knapweed burrs catch in car tires, dog muzzles, and hikers' socks, dispersing seed far and wide. Betraying the colonizer's tooth for assertion, they toxify their neighbors from the roots. We thought we were gaining higher ground now, though the fog thinned only to chill the breeze. Then from nearby, a raven wonked. At its most vacant, any landscape will sire a raven. My grandfather once tamed a crow to snatch donuts from his hand. Would a raven do likewise? You can hear them croak in the desert and on tundras, mountain peaks or plains, but to study a raven up close you need more patience than I have. Ravens fly like hawks, avoid cities, and call out when everything is still. They figure well in legend.

At last we could make out surrounding ranges. Late sun gleaned contrasts absent a moment before. We set our pace for a push to the summit, crunching snowcrust, noting colonies of *Opuntia* cactus, stretching our limbs in yellow light. I turned my head but I could see no raven. So I thought about a friend active in the men's movement who recommends the practice of animal mentorships. Finding one's totem animal can lead to insight, he says. Like spearmaking or bongos, it sounds diverting to me. But the appeal of ravens eludes any motive. They live by some faculty related to wit. And whatever they know, they don't strain to tell us. I stooped and fingered a cactus, unusual in these parts, but prickly as five o'clock shadow.

On top of Whiskey Dick, we wandered among radio equipment. Lichens fretted every stone. December's moon whitened in the east, while away to the north, snow began to pelt Wenatchee. Winter had come when a dark bird spoke. We watched Mount Adams take the sun.

Skiways

S OLITUDE OCCURS as one of those hyphens in life I look forward to, but inside of twenty-four hours I'm talking to myself. With my family out of town for a week, the choice between beer and videos and some less flaccid occupation hovered like the bad angel and the good, though the haloed one had yet to offer any concrete suggestion. Then it snowed. I wriggled into wool pants, dug the car out, and buttered my skis for the lonesome wilds.

Steering my wagon into a canyon west of town, nose close to the windshield, I fixed a sharp eye for pickups coming on the narrow lane between walls of snow. I punched in four-wheel drive at the flats where ranch houses back up to Manastash Creek. Second gear succeeded third. I bounced along past heavily padded bodies off-loading snowmobiles. Then the road climbed higher, crossing a creek and winding among powder-pasted cliffs and broad alluvial fans. An impressive denning cave gaped on my right—I braked for a peek at husks of organic litter scattered about the opening. Magpies puzzled over snowdrifts.

Peace and stillness would be mine if only I cut the engine, I thought. But as soon as I did, other, higher-pitched engines bellowed from the woods. I would have to find a ski trail farther into the outback. At mile twenty-two I pulled off in a wide space, heard motors coming my way, u-turned, then tried another opening in the firs at a distance. No luck, but—more tired of the car than wary of rough riders—I decided to assert myself on skis. Since nobody else of my ilk appeared, the usual antipathies between skiers and snowmobile clubs counted for little. I poled for a mile or more; helmeted figures roared from every glade. The woods belonged to them, they knew it, and my attempt to gain a footing must have seemed a laughable sideshow amid their carnival of noise. "There goes Ichabod Crane on toothpicks," I imagined my tormentors sneering. I retreated, slid my skis into the hatch, and drove back out. Putting discontent at bay, I tried to think of how I might yet recover the afternoon. My little car seemed to know the way. I sat back and watched farm houses glide past, their holiday lights of green, red, and blue painting bright dabs against the fields. Before long I was banking left into the golf course parking lot. Families milled about when I arrived; most had been out long enough to think of loading up sleds and skis and planning supper. But I had my eye on a distant figure windmilling against a hedge of evergreens. He was one of those Nordic snow gods who look as though they'd be hell on their mothers, having been born with skis attached.

I shot ahead directly, planting poles and pulling my body like a pent-up raft in a reach of whitewater. The first good ski of every winter happens like this: the tracks are laid, your blood yodels, you lean into your strokes like first love—then you plant your face in the snow. But still you charge again, for pulled muscles can be tricked into suppleness if you pay them no heed, and the next thing you know, you've circled the course three times and breathing feels like reincarnation.

The Nordic snow god glided up behind—he turned out to be an acquaintance—and while we exchanged words, the sun made miracles of cloud on Manastash Ridge. Behind us, the Yakima River all but swallowed highway clatter. After a while we parted, he toward the parking lot, I toward a knoll for Telemark practice, but from the margin of my sight I spied a robust grandmother watching me herringbone up the slope. From below she called, "Pretty neat!" then followed in the same fashion. I hope to move as limberly in thirty years.

Well, I had found my solitude and my society in the old Scandinavian sport of premotorized days, the best way still to make friends with snow and cool your cabin fever.

Biophilia

Love means I want you to be.
—St. Augustine, *The City of God*

HAVE YOU ever wondered why some of us prefer thickets, while for others the height of beauty is a manicured lawn? Or why, for that matter, some go to stock-car races while others commune at the zoo? Maybe there's a reason behind one man's passion for rivers and another's delight in hydro dams.

Edward O. Wilson thinks so. According to the prize-winning Harvard biologist, our genes predispose us to love the natural world. Having spent 99 percent of our history as hunter-gatherers, we have trained our senses to seek life-giving landscapes with water, mosaics of trees and open space, and long views—the better to find food, of course, or to survey approaching danger. It is likewise the ancestral environment that explains our affection for pets. Indeed, evolutionary fitness may have depended on our ability to value all of nature. Biophilia, says Wilson, is "the innately emotional affiliation of human beings to other living organisms."

In the verdant sheep and orchard country of northern Spain, Wilson's theory finds expression in the cave paintings of Altamira. Twelve thousand years ago, Europeans made animal images there and in similar sites whose emotive powers have never been surpassed. Even today, the pictographs at Altamira reward viewers with their gift of insight. I myself have had little experience of large, ungulate mammals, but observing "the Wounded Bison" with its legs collapsed beneath it, its powerful head lowered as if in supplication, I have felt the blood quicken in my limbs. Later, at a cafe table, I have pondered the integrity that must have linked the artist and this longed-for animal. In another panel, mixed herds of horned and antlered creatures gallop wildly in figure-eight patterns reminiscent of the infinity symbol. An enthusiasm not wholly lost to us revives at Altamira, as if we woke from dreams in a foreign language now understood as our own.

The past may unlock the origins of biophilia, but its relevance for the present is uncertain. Starved by the sensory diet of postmodern culture, never having hunted or gathered for a living, how can we lay claim to the responsiveness of our heritage? Several colleagues of Edward O. Wilson have considered the problem. By interviewing Seattle residents about their tree preferences, for example, Gordon Orians found that a clear partiality exists for particular species and growth patterns. Tellingly, the qualities most appreciated in height, width, and canopy layering are also typical of trees on the African savannah. Such biases once meant survival for fruit eaters and seekers of arboreal refuge. Researchers have also shown that natural settings—even a city courtyard of ginkgo trees—can stimulate the immune system as well as certain kinds of intelligence. Yet still other findings suggest that biophilia has gone beyond utility. Is it too obvious to suppose that people like nature because we are drawn to beauty? However that may be, Wilson has presented evidence attributing the best of human potential—our creativity, joy, attentiveness, and generosity—to intimacy with other species.

Conversely, Wilson argues, natural selection has taught us to fear nature's reptiles and venomous spiders. Most people still avoid blinding enclosures and deserts with little food. Some have called these reflexes "biophobia." It follows that sane individuals can easily distinguish between places that support life—eutrophic ponds, for instance—and those which discourage it, such as chlorinated swimming pools. In healthy people, biophilia and biophobia would function as twin ventricles of the heart.

Now here is where the theory gets dicey. If biophilia exists, then why aren't we a race of tree huggers? Given our ingrained sensitivity, we ought to feel chagrined when we suffocate wetlands under blacktop. But looking around us we see otherwise. The filmmaker Woody Allen speaks for many in his aversion to natural bodies of water, exclaiming, "There are living things in there!" In a similarly comic vein, signs posted on the campus where I work deter unwary walkers from patches of native rose and ryegrass. "DANGER, UNIMPROVED AREA," they say. "ENTER AT YOUR OWN RISK." Hazarding trespass anyway, I once confronted a grounds crew in the act of sawing down fine, old, black locust trees. "Aw, they're too messy," explained the foreman. Factor a global population together with attitudes like his and you get wholesale extinctions, soil and groundwater depletion, and attendant disasters too daunting to recite.

Not surprisingly, then, our environmental crisis is matched for scale only by the vehemence of those who deny it. We listen, dumbstruck, to conservative screeds against "pagan extremists" and "econazis," supposing they must refer to people like Edward O. Wilson, by all other accounts a gentle and cautious man. When violent rhetoric sways a public already panicked about economic collapse, Greens can count the corpses.

But if Wilson is right about biophilia, how have we come to such an impasse? Why would so many ignore their better nature? Wendell Berry, among others, has pointed out the fact that multiple generations now separate most Americans from the land. These days, the percentage of an average lifespan that is spent combing local fields and woodlots declines at about the same rate as open spaces themselves. A study reported by the botanist Gary Nabhan shows a weakened affinity for animals even among Native American kids. Unlike their elders, they have cut their teeth on a diet of video games and fast food. Wilson reminds us that biophilia is a seed. Time and opportunity are needed to make it grow, and in their absence it fails. When biophilia atrophies, biophobic apathy fills the void. Instead of habitat recovery, we get shopping, golf courses, and ORV proving grounds.

At some stage of analysis, the biophilia hypothesis must throw us back upon ourselves. If, as they say, ontogeny repeats phylogeny, then memory might teach us what we owe to the wild. I recall a box full of nestling grey squirrels I grieved for at age seven (their mother having been killed in the road) who suckled milk from the eyedropper I held and warmed themselves on a hot water bottle. Likewise, I remember my grandfather's beach house and the shingle-sided shed ensconced in rosa rugosa: inside, I would finger the handle of a clam rake and smell geraniums on the old man's work shirt—it draped like a frond of sea lettuce from an anchor tine bolted to the wall. Elsewhere, in my mind, I keep the far Norwegian heath where once a songbird counseled, "You-are-*welcome*-here. You-are-*not*-alone." Sifting autobiographical sands we can strive to be more worthy of the world, though in the long run we may best value the personal by finding ways to employ it.

Accordingly, many have sought to answer the anti-environmental challenge. Scientist Michael Soulé argues that awareness of biophilia *as an idea* could itself crack our cultural indifference. For evidence, he cites the fact that nonviolent civil disobedience, arising first as a concept, has fundamentally shaped the direction of Western politics. Likewise, the historian Roderick Nash proposes that just as political rights were granted first to African-American men, then to women, and finally to Native Americans, so in time will legal rights be extended to other species. Time, of course, is the operative word. The western hemisphere alone loses an estimated 140 species a day.

Perhaps more invigorating than scholarly speculation, though harder to come by directly, are the teachings of some native peoples. The anthropologist Richard Nelson describes the ways that Inuits learn not only to know animals, but also to know what animals have learned. Polar bears, for instance, have figured out how to hunt seals by waiting motionless on the downwind side of their breathing holes. Arctic indigenes do the same and credit the bear with teaching them. Far away in the Peruvian Andes live the Kogi Indians, whose testimony provided some of the first evidence of atmospheric thinning. For several decades now, the Kogis have witnessed climate changes in the decline of alpine plants around their homeland. Kogi mythology has also received attention. In one story, multitudes of pale-faced "younger brothers" steal their elder brother's inheritance, forcing him to live on inhospitable mountainsides while they despoil the fertile valleys below. Story blends with current event when the elder brother, isolated for generations, descends from his peaks to renew an ecological compact with his siblings. "The world does not have to end," says one Kogi elder, speaking to an Australian journalist. "If we act well, the world will go on."

Right behavior is the province of ethics, a curricular omission noted by many critics of public schools. Few among the more vocal, however, have acknowledged the crisis of extinction, an issue that E. O. Wilson places foremost among human concerns. To be sure, a limited biological stock bodes ill for all species. But lest "diversity" lapse into a cultural cliché, we have to somehow make it real.

My wife unwrapped a Tuscan loaf and boiled shrimp, remarking that, like everything else at Woodland Park Zoo, the table top we borrowed served instruction and pleasure alike. Cast into the table's bronze plane was a bas-relief map of North America, and into the map were etched the names of dead animals—the birds, fish, mammals, and others, dozen upon dozen, to whom we have been "a little more than kin and less than kind." We were spreading our feast across an atlas of extinction.

I won't claim that our shrimp lost their savor or that my appetite for salty bread abated. For that matter, no one I know of has actually died of grief at the Vietnam Memorial wall. But this is not to say that about our national heedlessness we are consoled. I forget who it was imagined hell as an endless hall of mirrors turned inward on the self, enforcing self-absorption for eternity. I don't know if it is lonelier still to picture a pine sapling in an erstwhile clearcut of fellow hybrids covering the earth to all horizons. But to live for human interest alone is vanity and an ecological fallacy. For biodiversity is not the province of Brazil or Alaska only, where the beauty of the world makes every plant and animal a paragon. Extinction is the name of our hometown, where developers crow the advent of their watch. Remember the bluebirds where that strip mall just went in? Watch for them next year and count their absences.

Professor Wilson feels that we need not absent ourselves, that we can reclaim our membership in nature. But our best chance of derailing the extinction train, he believes, may have little to do with affection. Calling upon the evolutionary value of self-interest, Wilson urges that we protect biodiversity because wild things give us raw materials. Nature provides medicines, you know, and fossil-fuel substitutes. It seems that in political circles, mere happiness and spiritual health butter no turnips. And so, knowing better, we settle for pragmatism in hopes of saving a species or two. But love is the gist of biophilia, whatever else we make of it.

Part III

Wondering

AFTER MONTHS of low fog and hoarfrost, we feel like seals trapped under an ice floe, searching in vain for a breathing hole. Cloudy weather so blurs the valley that we begin to doubt whether our mountains are still present out there, or whether some twitch of plate tectonics has carried them away. You would think that out of sight meant well in mind where the North Cascades are concerned. They are young, glaciated upthrusts vivid enough to charge one's memory for a lifetime. Yet I have learned to acknowledge apathy, a weakness common enough at high latitudes in February, but well known everywhere. I once washed dishes with a man who had lived beside the Grand Canyon for twenty years. "Shit, I never look at that damn thing," he told me. "It ain't nothing but a big, brown hole." I swore if I ever took to his point of view I'd turn cartwheels off the South Rim. I suggested some such remedy to my co-worker, who showed little interest in recovering his sense of wonder.

Here in central Washington, far from the international tourist trade and the knipsing of camera springs, landmarks can be properly valued. When, after a long hiatus, the clouds lift and Mt. Stuart appears, people in the Kittitas crane their necks and breathe to the diaphragm. Our big peaks convert the skeptic in us, whether by some alchemy of joy or by their sheer, aspiring presence. Impatient to shake off boredom as I drive out west of town today, I watch them rising above the foothills as brilliantly unfazed as the Hindu pantheon.

Sun on powder snow, powder flocking boughs, hedgerows, thickets, telephone wires, and country people's eyebrows—these sights have drawn me to Robinson Canyon for a tour in late winter. I haven't skied a mile, though, when a cyclone fence interrupts the trail. For a while I've been scenting tanned leather and road apples. I notice now that aspens hereabouts are rough and blackened as far up their trunks as a grazing animal might gnaw. Up ahead, gliding bands of camel-like ungulates forage mounds of feed and shy along the forest fringe. They are does and calves mostly, yet I see the occasional bull among them, too; I'd like to move closer but a sign says, "No access during feeding season." I have breasted the frontier of an elk zoo. It seems that local herds survive the winter on Wildlife Department hand-outs, a concept weird to wilderness lovers, but one fated by development of all the best habitat. "By every conceivable measure, humanity is ecologically abnormal," says the scientist E.O. Wilson. Our management of other species confirms this view, though I don't see a fix for the problem. Nor do I see any way to ski in Robinson Canyon today. Instead I watch the elk.

More properly called wapiti, these are extravagant creatures that bark when alarmed, squeal out of tenderness, and blare like trumpets during courtship. So passionate is their rut that as many as a third of all bulls in a herd may burn out from the strain, retiring to cool their frenzy in mud wallows before they die. Elk will really trash a piece of landscape, too. Broken saplings, girdled trees, and uprooted shrubs are signs of them rubbing the velvet off their antlers and polishing them for show. At other times of year they appear almost bucolic. I have seen young elk cavorting in a high-country pond in summer with as much abandon as kids on a Fourth-of-July picnic. I admire their foolery then, splashing and butting heads, churning the water and shaking it off their hides like stick-chasing labs. For humans the alternative is often cynicism, so let there be gusto instead. Today feels like the moment of stasis just before winter cracks. In a few weeks, the snow I travel on will have joined the Columbia River, and these big deer will follow warm air currents to higher ground. I watch them feed until one foot falls asleep. A wish for beguilement brings me on this errand, but I may have to settle for aerobics. Turning away from the fence, I resume the kick-and-glide striding that brought me here, happy to be exercised without motivational tapes, gratified as I chafe off the final globs of last April's klister wax.

Now there comes a sight for pained eyes in the shape of a great raptor wheeling above the cliffs. It's an eagle, judging by that breadth of wing; a bald eagle by the white fan tail and snowy head. Mottled undersides show the bird's emergence from youth, but make no mistake, this is the creature that somehow edged out the turkey for the honor of national totem. How splendidly and with what economy of effort the eagle soars. As an embodiment of self-confidence and prowess, its place in American iconography is secure. Yet Westerners once killed eagles in droves, believing them predators of sheep, and some still do hate them enough to break the law. (It is a fact that the birds eat only stillborn lambs and the afterbirths of cows.) DDT residues hamper reproduction in many regions, yet bald eagles are holding their own in the Northwest.

Now a second eagle appears, dive-bombing the first, and I watch, amazed, as they plummet out of sight. Balds pass through the Kittitas Valley only as migrants, they say. But what I've just seen resembles nothing so much as a courtship dance, renowned for being conducted mid-air with the talons of each partner locked together. Is this pair an anomaly, intending to remain here and nest? Is the mottled bird even old enough to mate? Whatever I'm watching, I interpret it as excellence. We may never plumb the depths of conversation with other animals, yet we can sense a kinship in their will to live ardently.

The younger eagle reappears from behind a craggy Douglas fir. I think of the time I observed a group of school kids being introduced to a wolf. There were sixty children in a gym with echo-chamber acoustics, but the only audible sounds were of breathing and hushed, happy sighs. As the wolf circled the aisles, licking hands and smelling the shoes of so many human pups, the children seemed to radiate pleasure. Wild wonders are harder to arrange, it's true. Yet here in Robinson Canyon I find elation soaring on wide wings. My last glimpse affords an image of the eagle's bill. It's a massive weapon wrought for tearing flesh, as big as the paws of a wolf.

Returning to my car, I remember reading a scholarly study about parent-and-child book reading. Some adults give their kids a straight read, discouraging interruptions and posing no questions themselves. Others behave as raconteurs, digressing from the text for conversation and prompting their kids to respond. Researchers found that children exposed to the second style of reading learned as a matter of habit to ask more questions, generally, and to raise more complex questions in particular. On the contrary, kids used to straight readings came to perceive knowledge as unambiguous, a substance to be poured into empty vessels. Straight readers learned obedience.

Stimulated by elk and eagles, I find myself hoping for a time when the ability to wonder gains stature among basic competencies. That would be a fine day for school children and, perhaps, for what we call nature. Until then, I hold with the poet who said of love that it "begins in delight and ends in wisdom." This is a proverb befitting students of the wild.

Backlash

I DIDN'T WANT to think about enemies as I picked my way back from the mailbox. Terry Tempest Williams has called the environmental movement "a loving embrace," and I can't deny the wisdom of her words. But at the moment I speak of I was trying to keep my footing in the slick river that mud season makes of our driveway, and I couldn't very well reflect. The pamphlet I'd received called up thoughts of Green-hating legislators, their industry sponsors, and the threats they pose to natural communities. As I enter middle age, "deregulation" is the word. But trashing landscapes—and, as I've learned, the land's defenders—is the deed in fashion. By the time I reached my doorstep I wanted vengeance.

A group calling themselves "the Committee for Environmental Justice" was urging postal patrons to fight a plan that would link U.S. and Canadian national parks. Never mind the benefits of intact ecosystems; the pamphlet warned that the core of one of these parks would have *no people in it!* and that this fact implied a conspiracy to found a one-world government, religion, and economy.

Though drizzle accounted for the water on my face, outrage might as well have done the drenching. I recalled similar epistles I'd received, including one from a "Christian-oriented" property rights group assuring me that the Endangered Species Act is ungodly, since it often foils our injunction to subdue the earth and exercise authority over the lilies of the field. For a nest of crossed wires, religious reactionism surpasses all. The Bible has carried its word through two or three millennia of linguistic change (passing through four or five languages en route) and so, for that reason if not others, I can trace in it no reliable and consistent guide to land use.

As interpretive mysteries go, the Bible has been outdone during the 1990s only by congressional policy-making, which aims to liberate us from the hair shirt of emissions control, pesticide restrictions, and mandatory double hulls on oil tankers. Does anyone remember "the Jobs Creation Act"? Another coinage worthy of dystopian fiction, the bill failed to pass the Senate but ended up sending green laws to the cleaners by way of add-on riders.

Some nature bashers mince words; others confine their damage to fish and trees. Where they find common ground is in their weakness for paranoia. Holy rolling and isolationism account for part of this trend, but most popular, because most immediately threatening, has been the appeal to economics. "Why," asks industry lobbyist Ron Arnold, "do these environmentalists want to destroy our free enterprise system?" According to Arnold, opposition to clearcutting shows an elitist contempt for working families, and besides, the national forest system itself is obviously "a socialist arrangement." In Arnold's mind, environmentalists are "the new pagans," and the only way to revive America is to cut down their sacred groves.

But the real difficulty posed by conspiracy theories is that they sometimes have teeth. What do we make of the Deep South before civil rights, when Klansmen walked free after lynching blacks? What shall we say of our late presidential wire tapper, Richard Nixon, or of Karen Silkwood, murdered while blowing the whistle on nuclear polluters? In a documentary called *The War Against the Greens*, David Helvarg dredged up evidence of organized terrorism that should make the most humble Audoboner think twice before opening the mailbox. According to Helvarg, the perpetrators of anti-environmentalism have included a predictable assortment of angry sociopaths and shadowy, corporate underwriters; for victims they've usually targeted women, Indians, student interns, and anyone else unlikely to be armed. If we accept Helvarg's account—and his documentation is impeccable—anybody publicly espousing conservation may qualify for telephone harassment, death threats, and even more chilling forms of mayhem. Here are a few of their stories.

In 1989, Paula Siemers of Cincinnati lost her son to a rare form of leukemia. Suspecting emissions from factories in her neighborhood (one had been cited for forty hazardous waste violations), Siemers began organizing protest marches. In the wake of a petition drive, she found hate notes pinned to her front door. Rocks were thrown through her windows at night, one of which knocked her young daughter unconscious. Then the family dog was poisoned. After speaking with a *Sixty Minutes* reporter, Siemers was attacked, beaten, and stabbed. Eventually, the poor woman fell ill with post-traumatic stress disorder and went into hiding under an assumed name.

In 1993, Navajo environmentalist Leroy Jackson was hung in effigy at a pro-logging rally in New Mexico. He had become active in the forest preservation movement after vandals ransacked his family's ancestral hogan and hijacked dozens of old trees nearby. Later, three days before he was to have testified before Congress against further cutting, Jackson turned up dead in his van. Officials ruled the death a suicide by drug overdose, though friends described the deceased as an optimistic, clean-living man. State police never did resolve conflicts in witness testimony.

A year before Leroy Jackson died, Adirondack preservationist Anne La Bastille came home to find her house burned down.

Police called the fire arson, but they never arrested suspects in the case, nor did they find the vandals who destroyed a local conservation office the same night. A bomb strapped beneath her car maimed Judi Barry, another single woman, who was attacked while organizing California's Redwood Summer. The FBI at first blamed Barry herself for transporting the bomb, and while charges against her were later dropped, no one was ever brought to justice.

Confronted with stories like these, one debates whether to feel more discouraged by the attacks themselves or by the lukewarm efforts made to account for them. As reported by Helvarg, during the same year that Paula Siemers was stabbed, shrimper/conservationist Diane Wilson found that her boat had been sunk, Greenpeace scientist Pat Cosner's house was torched, and dozens of other environmentalists were shot at, forced off the road, and beaten. Yet the FBI reported that "there were no suspected terrorist incidents" during the period these incidents occurred. Higher up the chain of command, Ronald Reagan's former interior secretary, James Watt, advocates open season on Greens: "If the troubles from environmentalists cannot be solved in the jury box or at the ballot box, perhaps the cartridge box should be used." This is the sort of talk that accounts for a great many unlisted telephone numbers.

Anti-green violence seems anomalous in a country where, according to several studies, a clear majority consider themselves environmentalists. It makes more sense in light of the sources that stand behind it. South African mining concerns, Japanese ORV makers, and the Unification Church have all contributed to Ron Arnold's "Wise Use" organization. And despite their pseudo-populist moniker, the "People for the West" number twelve mining executives among their thirteen original members. Still, the proponents of green backlash will aim for respectability in the long run, for statistics suggest that earth love is a mainstream phenomenon. Eighty-two percent in a Times-Mirror poll favored "stricter laws to protect the environment," and sixty-seven percent said they would pay higher prices for them.

Of course, many of these are voters who endorsed the deregulatory onslaught when it first began, a conundrum that leaves me as unsettled now as I felt while pausing beside my mailbox, ankle-deep in mud and pulling knapweed riders from my pant cuffs. Why would citizens who say they value nature elect officials hostile to the land? Will doublespeak always prevail? Pardon me while I defuse my mailbox.

Blewett Pass Valentine

To WEATHER A change needed little more than a change in the weather this week. Chiming Bohemian waxwings retreated to the woods, having stripped the last chokecherry from rural hedgerows, while in town, the icicles grinning from house eaves began to crumble. Insulation tradespeople can smile their way through winter, but many of us feel restless. The slumbers of holiday time are past. We lose heart for hanging around the supper table, and as with wakeful groundhogs, fits of expectancy turn my family outdoors in even the most drenching air. After all, maybe the clouds are breaking up. We have to see for ourselves.

My wife, my young son, and I approached Blewett Pass through a swirl of dollar-sized nitrogen pies that made the pretense of being snow. Were it not for the fact of a broken windshield wiper, the disguise might have fooled us. As it happened, we waxed our skis for wetness and entered the trees in the spirit you bring to such occasions: it's better to go out and take your licks than to wait for Hawaiian weather. Still, what a pelting we got! I felt like a mayfly trapped in a field of exploding dandelion puffs. The liquid snow (or viscous rain—they call it Cascade cement) took seconds to saturate our anoraks. I could have used wipers on my glasses, even broken ones, but I settled for shortsighted steerage and the whiff of hazard.

Our trail promised "intermediate" difficulty according to the diamond blazes nailed to tree trunks. We dismissed that adjective as soon as the snow had so glommed our skis that every glide stroke felt like toil. But after a while we got used to awkwardness. The path, which started by heading uphill to an open slope and then idling along a skid road to the right, next began to twist and mosey through tight spaces among the pines. Any but the crudest turns were out of the question. We resorted to a panicky style of skiing familiar to those who learn to do it in the woods. If slush clogs your stride, you stagger. When ice hurtles you headlong down an incline, you thrust both poles between your legs and drag, or failing that, let your keister brake the slide. It's softer than your head.

On top of a snikkerty knoll we paused to hear chickadees lisping a two-note mating call. Theirs is a simple song made interesting by the fact that they deliver it at any time of year, whether they feel frisky or not. Still, they use no other call when they really mean business. "*Phee-per!*" There it was, a valentine from Blewett Pass. For such a potent urge, sex plays cat and mouse with chickadees as much as it does with people. We may fiddle with details, but the rule of mystery holds: you never know where you'll end up when you set about swapping genes.

We didn't know where we were going either. Our day resembled Limburger cheese, which we savor for nearly provoking disgust. The snow turned to rain and then to sleet. Branches eased it from their backs, filling the woods with the sound of a bunkhouse pillow fight. We counted as lucky every *whump* that missed us when it fell. Soon, we closed our loop at the skid road.

"Welcome all dozing groundhogs," we pledged, "from the back doors of your hollows. Sample the air with us a while. Savor the atoms we do. Give the neighborhood a whisker twitch. Think about mating; take a nap."

Tying the Knot

POSTMARKED Cashmere, Washington, the letter was written to protest the Green movement's "pagan spiritualism," a phenomenon I had seemed to endorse in a radio commentary. Identifying herself as a "concerned Christian," my correspondent said, "environmentalists religionize their movement, not understanding that it is just a political movement." Moreover, she continued, "it is detrimental to give it religious foundations and overtones." Curiously, the writer omitted any grounds for her argument. Perhaps, like much public discourse in America, hers was put forth without expectation of dialogue. During reactionary times, to say what one thinks is to know.

Apart from knowing then, what I *believe* is that whether God exists in nature or, as many Christians suppose, somewhere else, Higher Power Itself may be less concerned with opinions than behavior. Gary Snyder describes our historical moment in terms of a "post-industrial, pre-collapse" society, one whose condition might have been foretold in the Book of Isaiah:

> The earth mourns and withers,
> the world languishes and withers;
> the heavens languish together
> with the earth.
> The earth lies polluted
> from the touch of its inhabitants;
> for they have transgressed the laws...

Despite the scriptural prevalence of such passages, the powerful Christian Coalition has adopted the same stance as my correspondent. Their spokesman insists that his group "takes no position on the environment." He may be telling a literal truth, but of course, to profess neutrality on the fundamental problem of the Holocene epoch is to endorse the status quo. No one knows how much longer a posture of disinterest can be affected. But the ecological disasters now pending are serious enough to warrant the conclusion of Hildegard of Bingen, a medieval anchorite, that "God's justice permits creation to punish humanity." In any event, the delusion of conservative Christians is perplexing. Wendell Berry has pointed out the absurdity of being obsessed with bodily resurrection while sanctioning abuses of the body's source. Unfortunately, the religious right no longer limit themselves to passive aggression. Many who wear the cross of Jesus seem as immune to charity as to reason. Bashing gay people, demonizing environmentalists, they remind me of those early monotheists who would atone for their own sins by driving some harassed, unlucky beast into the Dead Sea. Ritual scapegoating will surely intensify as our crises deepen. Blame has often been the currency of social disintegration. In the absence of common ground, hostility toward some Other is one of the few ways left for people to bond. Call it natural selection or original sin, the cult of enemies justified the twentieth century's many schemes for racial purification. Given the sordidness of precedent, perhaps tree huggers will one day wear earth symbols stitched to their lapels.

The Green movement has come of age, and in response, neoconservatives have adopted some pretty sinister rhetoric. Idaho congresswoman Helen Chenoweth, for one, outstripped my Cashmere correspondent by declaring a "holy war" on environmentalists. Though the immediate victims of congressional jihad are land, water, and air, it must be admitted that Chenoweth paid her enemies the compliment of a sincere regard. Likewise, the Reverend Sun Myung Moon (who thinks he is God) keeps covenant by bankrolling anti-enviro's such as the "Wise Use" organization, more properly known as Unwise Abuse. Even the billionaire Moon, a convicted felon, has identified Greens as a spiritual force. But I am wrong to identify the woman from Cashmere with fascistic power brokers. It's my solstice bonfires that trouble her, not my Greenpeace credentials. I wish I could ease conservative fears about druids and Halloween. But how do we discuss the difference between New Age folderol (which is probably harmless enough in most respects) and the true promptings of the heart? Picture, for example, an October morning on Icicle Creek: a circle of friends lifting voices under leaf fall; a drum beat driving out bitterness, welcoming joy and fidelity—are these to be explained or justified?

It comes as no surprise that nature religion offends many Christians. For centuries their forerunners suffered not the witch to live among them, and the witch, as we learn from the Reformation's annals, was anyone whose path through the woods good Christians feared to follow. Pantheists never indulge in religious warfare, yet crusades are the fundamentalist's dietary staple.

Admittedly, no tradition has proven immune to human prejudice. It's just that the metaphors of adversity—Satan, for example—have meant more to some traditions than others. Generation after generation, tribal impulses foster bigotry as surely as steam rising from snowmelt. Still, that is not to say we should purge our emotions, even if doing so were possible. Passion can serve reasonable ends. When I learned that my well had been tainted by agricultural chemicals, and that my family had been innocently drinking poison, I needed no feat of insight to imagine the same water polluting a baptismal font. Caring for nature, I've learned, entails many acts of devotion.

A similar conviction is found wherever hope is alive. Wangari Maathai, a leader of Kenya's Green Belt Movement, has gone farther than most in enacting an ecologically inspired faith.

By organizing tens of thousands of women and children to plant over seven million trees in East Africa, Maathai is helping to reverse deforestation. And since Kenyan women grow most of their country's food, she has led them in forming sustainable business and community partnerships. An interviewer asked Maathai why she became an environmentalist, prompting her to answer, "All of us have a God in us, and that God is the spirit that unites all life—everything that is on this planet. And it must be this voice that is telling me to do something. And I am sure it is the same voice that is speaking to everybody...concerned about the fate of the world."

Like Ghandi, King, and other great humanitarians, Wangari Maathai is religious. The difference is that more and more voices like hers are speaking out of the belief that all life is sacred. Following their example, we may yet discover that our dealings with the earth imply the most ancient covenant of every faith. The Dalai Lama of Tibet has argued that it is futile to separate social concerns, environmentalism being the most vital, from what we call religion. Since his exile following the Chinese invasion, he has worked to restore his homeland's status as a peaceful Buddhist country. "It is my dream," he writes, "that the entire Tibetan plateau should become a free refuge where humanity and nature can live in harmonious balance." Several years ago, the Dalai Lama persuaded Pope John Paul II to meet and discuss issues of "world peace, spiritual values and protection of the earth's natural environment." While it is true that the Pope obstructs population control, he, too, has argued for environmental ethics, calling the human treatment of nature a moral crisis.

In *The End Of Nature*, Bill McKibben argues that nature as we've known it throughout evolution is, in a manner of speaking, gone. Urbanized landscapes, synthetic food, and artificial time have in fact replaced our ancestral environment. That being the case, nature religion becomes more of a challenge in practice than fundamentalists may appreciate. How do we celebrate lunar phases when city lights render them invisible? Shall we toast the harvest with BHT-altered cows' milk?

Against all odds, however, many people find delight in the richness of life remaining. Water fowl migrations along the Columbia River may be dwarfed by those of the past, but to the appreciative observer they are wonderful still. And despite rampant development, the persistence of flowering balsamroots near my home in the Kittitas Valley is a sight to awaken gratitude. According to the Bible, the earth has been, and can be, a life-giving cornucopia. Even with our agriculture failing and species going extinct by the thousands—or perhaps because of these tragedies—the words of the prophets pass current yet:

> O Lord, how manifold are your works!
> In wisdom you have made them all;
> the earth is full of your creatures.
> Yonder is the sea, great and wide,
> creeping things innumerable are there,
> living things both small and great.
> These all look to you
> to give them their food in due season;
> when you give it to them, they gather it up;
> when you open your hand, they are filled with good things.

This is surely the one in whom we all "live and move and have our being." Is it possible, as some claim, that God is losing sleep over details of social decorum?

Some go to church, some go to the woods. *Religare,* the Latin root of "religion," means "to bind together separate strands." Committed to life-giving acts, people of all faiths may learn to overstep the barriers of habit. Ecology is the tying of the knot.

Observatory

I F YOU'VE NEVER actively anticipated love or mosquitoes, you may guess for yourself how often the hum surpasses the sting. I've known both kinds of bug. Attribute my weakness to character if appearances tell truly, but the distance between expectation and fact is one I strain to account for. Taken as a maxim, the uncertainty principle applies to back-country bushwacking as well. We seldom get where we plan to go by following our noses, my wife and I, a likelihood that guides Lori's faith in clear directions. Out on the trail, maps and charted routes allow her to welcome each moment collectedly. I myself am attracted to drama. Earth tremors, predatory mammals, heat lightning, anything hairy or sudden speaks to my ken. I do fear the side effects of danger though, so I have agreed to wander from local paths only by way of compensation. All I ask is that they be sufficiently obscure. Lori takes issue with my preference, and that is the reason of this tale.

On a clear day, if you find yourself situated in the Kittitas Valley, your eyes can scroll the length of knobby Manastash Ridge, a dry, perpendicular outrunner of the Cascade Range. When the occasion is right, you will see a white node peering from the trees like a monocle beneath raised eyebrows. This is the University of Washington observatory. I had climbed the ridge for wildflowers in April and constellations in July, but so far I had let myself be sidetracked from a destination that now seemed essential. "We are as much as we see," Thoreau confided to his journal. Near the end of an overcast winter, his sentiment seemed especially tailored to my mind. "Well, then let's do an observatory trip," said Lori. The morning in late February when I accepted her proposal was mild, and it promised sunshine if the fog lifted. With snowmelt quickening, we would seize our last opportunity to ski the ridge.

Our tour began where Manastash Creek burbles among riparian hardwoods. We climbed an unmarked trail between pillars of pock-marked basalt, sapling evergreens projecting from tenuous rootholds at our elbow. Before we had time to lose our breath, views began opening eastward. Our spirits rise whenever tree cover thins, especially when we seek reprieve from winter shadows. But my wife and I are apprentice Northwesterners, and I credited the regional tonic for much of the pleasure we felt. Two cups of strong coffee had equipped my joints with gyroscopes and little rubber bearings. I was striding along on the grease of self-satisfaction and talking too much. Lori took my arm at one point, and with her free hand touched her ski pole to a hemlock fingerling growing from a nurse log. It seemed a short climb, as I recovered my modesty, from caffeine to reverence.

Our forest road followed the contours of the land at one stretch, the convenience of departed loggers at another, but it raveled ever upward through cryptic basins, blow-down glens, and deer yards. Then, two miles along, our baby carrier collapsed. An aluminum spar poked me in the ribs, and my little boy hung at a three-quarter angle from the wreckage. What to do? I fiddled with shoelacing while Lori served juice and crackers. When my repairs failed, I yanked free the offending piece of aluminum and proposed we keep going. Erik gave little wren-like cheeps, delighted to experiment with gravity, as it seemed to me. It would be a pity to abandon the trip, Lori conceded, as one brought to act against judgment but inclined to bank her veto for use in an emergency. I commented on signs of feeding I saw, figuring to varnish doubt with distraction. Here we found the bark of an elderberry shrub peeled off in strips, and nearby, gnaw-patterns engraving young ponderosas. Deer and elk were taking their famine food. I held up a knot of wolf lichens for inspection. When scalawag Lori suggested a taste test, I felt obliged to comply. It worked the jaws like coarse parsley, as nearly flavorless as tofu.

A series of turns put the height of land within striking distance. But attempts to reach it by several spur trails brought us no closer. After all, timbermen go where trees can be had, while our destination poked above the trees. Having skied this far we should find a way to skiddle up, I argued, come whatever may. Had we not set out to reach the observatory by an unexplored route? Wouldn't it be sublime to pilgrim our way haphazardly, arriving at the temple of starsplitters after trials of initiation? Lori didn't contend. She spoke to Erik, now hanging almost perpendicular from the baby carrier. I felt a cluster of scrimshander's knots beginning to clench my back. We scaled the final half-mile without benefit of a path.

On top of the ridge at last, I deemed our pluck rewarded. Cornsnow popped beneath our skis, and the first truly warm sunshine of the year gave Manastash Ridge the look of a winter garden. We glided eastward among meadows and stunted firs, basking in affinities I couldn't trace. This was not the landscape of my formative years. The ridge had never appeared to me in a dream. How to explain its charmed appeal? Richard Leakey, the anthropologist, links the popularity of parklands to our African origins. Taking the Manastash as evidence, grassy acres interspersed with groves delight the natives of Kittitas County as much as they do a native Kenyan. Responses to landscapes may be echoes of the past.

The observatory beckoned distantly when we finally caught sight of it. I had figured on coming out close by. Still, it couldn't be more than a couple of miles along, and the sun shone strongly yet at three o'clock. So along we skied, prize-eyed man, woman and child deep in talk. We had exchanged loads by this time. I carried the food and extra mittens while Erik draped himself across his mother like some poorly dispatched quarry.

An hour later, the observatory eluded us still. Our shadows grew horizonward. Then Lori found a descending logging road, and after coming within a mile of my grail I consented to give it up. Bulldozers had cleared the road for tree hauling. We carried our skis, hoping for a quick return as Erik began to whimper from the cold and afternoon retreated into winter. Impressions made under twilight and the strain of fatigue seemed fleeting now—a deer kill hollowed by coyotes, an orange moon rising through Ellensburg's inversion haze—but these appearances revived us for the final push.

Later on, riding home in the car, we felt that, however unexpectedly, we had gathered distances into ourselves. Perhaps we knew something more of astronomy now. At least, we could imagine peering from the eye in the sky on Manastash Ridge.

Ridge Walk

VIEWED FROM AN office window in my town, the summit of Umtanum Ridge wears a hoary, dark-green muffler. Its pine trees resemble grazing buffalo herds, which never roamed here, or the bighorn sheep and wapiti that do. Their habitat is grassland folded over coulees and thrust upward to nigh 5,000 feet. The wildness they congregate is naked space. But a short ride from downtown plants your shoes among the roots of a billion angiosperms, the flowering plants that make our life possible.

Everything rooted lay quiet. Too late for snow, too soon for blossoms, I followed a dirt track upward from the valley. My sense of entering a different world was keen, for I knew I drove no ordinary byway—travelers once rode through here aboard a stagecoach bound for Yakima. Tasting the grit of a spring gale or a summer breeze, our great-grandparents would have seen much that I saw today. They would have watched Mt. Rainier compose the far horizon like the arms of a drawing compass. They would have viewed lowland towns as a pattern of jots and creases. Whatever their errand, coach riders must have shaped their thoughts to the openness of the country, perhaps envying the knowledge of native people. The Yakama guardians of this land may still be seen gathering plants hereabouts.

Downshifting in a gully, I noticed a sack of hogs' heads bounced or thrown from a truck. Magpies were picking them over, crowding each other as they vied for nutrition. Not one to witness such a scene without reaching for some sort of lesson, I thought I should look on and browse this chapter in the tale of nature's economy. But I realized I was only sightseeing.

When I parked the car I found a walking path just opposite three towers of crenelated basalt, rocks formed by ancient lava flows. Lichens now make soil of them. Still, I thought the rocks exerted enough impersonal force to panic a theologian. Exclaims a pilgrim in *The Canterbury Tales*,

> In ydel, as men seyn, ye no thyng make.
> But Lord, thise grisly feendly rokkes blake,
> That semen rather a foul confusion
> Of werk than any fair creacion
> Of swich a parfit wys God and a stable,
> Why han ye wroght this werk unresonable?

I dismissed as equally reasonless my urge to make nature signify, as in their way, so would the packrats that shelter in cliffs like these.

On the trail at last, I shuffled past alder thickets already tipped with buds. These "weed trees" still meet with disdain and herbicidal relatives of Agent Orange at the hands of timber companies. More recently, naturalists have lauded the alder's fertilizing gifts, and in an enlightened forestry, they would be encouraged on cut-over land. Picture the tree at work, its roots flexing little nodules within the soil like the knots on Popeye's arms. Masters of conversion, these buds draw nitrogen from the air and broadcast it through neighboring soil.

Back up on the prairie, sight and sensibility recovered their broader scope. Planes of hillside, sky, and distant ridge cut across one another and grew more startling as I climbed, so that I paused, one knee crooked and one straight like a Swiss cow, and bending at the waist, peered back through my legs. The ridgetops are a thrill viewed upside down or otherwise. I was happy to be here, where the fact that we live on a planet ruled by physical laws is indisputable.

Tramping the ridge required no map. It was up for wind and distance, down for quiet close-ups. Either way I found objects bright with color: "grey" bitterbrush fairly shuddered with royal blue and violet; alder buds waved Mexican flags. Beneath my soles, I felt the mile-long rhizomes of bunchgrass beginning to flex.

A Child in the Bush

AMONG THE CITIZENS of spring that day were yellow bells, the first wildflower of the prairie, and poking out beneath their namesake, sagebrush buttercups. Hills above the canyon sprouted green-gold shoots as fresh as the scent of baby's heads.

My pack-riding, one-year-old boy and I left Umtanum Canyon at the site of a ghost ranch, its tumbled stock pens and apple trees long since reverted to wild tenancy. We climbed a branch canyon rising to the south, and from above we saw pasture gone to rabbitbrush and colonies of aspen. Decades earlier, homesteaders had abandoned this site, and however it may have happened, their passing bid the inevitable reflection: *sic transit gloria mundi*, so it goes. But I've looked at scenes like this all of my growing-up years. In the woods of New England, lilacs and day lilies mark the edges of old cellar hole depressions under the leaves. When I wax melancholy, my thoughts are not of the past. Instead, I pity my child's grandchildren for the sights they will gaze on in the century to come.

Our climb pursued a narrow path made tortuous by the incline despite the number of tracks preceding ours. I could trace cleft pairs of sheep prints with my finger, noting how the spaces between them widened to accommodate purchase—bighorns are masterful mountaineers. We followed as best we could on size ten wafflestompers.

Today I had promised myself to be guided by my little boy. As soon as our crevasse eased onto the plain, I touched him down among sagebrush. Erik began the concentric wanderings of a fifteen-month baby-tod while I surveyed the distance through field glasses. Fresh droppings marked the earth at intervals, and I thought we might catch sight of coil-headed rams distracted by the sun. Then a hawk screamed its war cry. Songbirds scattered in panic, but Erik took up keening in his fancy for the raptor and bolted toward the cliff we had just overtopped. I snatched him clear in plenty of time. Still, it was all I could do amid the boy's fisticuffs to drag him out of harm's way.

"Deece?" inquired Erik, pointing out the "two-*Cree*-wives-in-a-wickiup" melody of the meadowlark. When he scuttered away again, I stood upright in order to keep him in view among the bushes. After six months of self-locomotion, he'd learned nothing of fear. Scouting Erik about to bury his hands in an ant colony, I swung him too roughly into my pack. He raged in protest, digging his tiny shoe soles into my kidneys and caterwauling. "All right, then," I shouted, "see how you like independence." On impulse, I set him down and strode away through the brush.

Was it passion I obeyed or a teachable moment? As a first-time parent I take informal guilt readings at every opportunity. But it was only later that I framed the question in a memory. A long time ago, my grandfather had a pond near his home in the woods. He kept a flock of Muscovy ducks there, though it was a trial, he said, to guard them from predators; and he worried so much about drowned grandchildren that I heard him on several occasions vowing to bulldoze the pond. I must have been three or four years old at the time, and I loved to wander away from the adults and chase the ducks around the shore of that black water overhung with hemlock trees. Yet the pond remained. One day I was dipping for frogs with a net when a snapping turtle, broad as a washtub, thrust its head above the surface and seized the bamboo shaft I held. I dropped the net and ran, screaming, along the path to the house. The next thing I remember is watching my grandfather bury the corpse of the huge reptile, which he had killed with a shovel. After that, I played behind the wood pile until I had learned to swim. I didn't have to be told.

Now, as I crouched out of sight observing Erik, I resolved that he, too, should discover separation anxiety. Since the primary lesson in staying alive doesn't come naturally in my family, I would design a prompt. Purposefully, I waited for Erik to react to my absence, the sage rich in my nose, a fritillary butterfly fanning its wings nearby. But all I could hear were sing-song and the scraping of feet. Three minutes: nothing. Five minutes: something. Duckwalking to gain the slope, Erik upended himself repeatedly. It hurt to fall face-first. And no, I wasn't there to help. Betrayal shook my baby boy's outcry—it was a sound I would rather not ever hear again. Still I waited a moment longer, playing Abraham to my son's Isaac, and trying to offer kindness behind a mask of cruelty. At last I rose and reached my arms to him.

Trespass and the Commons

*Possibly the day will come...when fences shall be
multiplied, and man-traps and other engines invented
to confine man to the public road, and walking over the
surface of God's earth shall be construed to mean
trespassing on some gentleman's grounds.*
—Henry David Thoreau, "Walking," 1862

PORT MEADOW, near the town of Oxford, England, is a broad floodplain beside the River Thames. Norman conquerors long ago felled the oaks that grew there, and farmers have grazed livestock among their ghosts ever since. But foxes, partridges, and badgers live there, too. No fences divide Port Meadow's acreage of grass and tree-lined shore. You can see old men angling for bream at water's edge. Skylarking students and Romany gypsies ply the Thames in barges, free to camp in the meadow by night. (I once watched a man in harlequin pants eating fire while his family ate stew.) Citizens with sketch pads, birding glasses, and rucksacks can walk for miles in either direction. Port Meadow is a commons.

The practice of setting land aside for wildlife and scot-free human use has been widespread in northern Europe. In early America, the same pattern held for a while as in their mutually hostile fashion Abenaki Indians and New England Yankees both endorsed the liberty of the commons. The city of Boston has always called its central park "the Common," and a scarcity of posted notices still makes for open entry to the hills of Vermont. I used to spend summer days there among beech and maple groves. Even where I did pass by signs withholding hunting rights, in many cases the landowner had blacked out the attendant phrase, "No Trespassing."

The story of these places is not the story of the far West, where I live now. Yet their history speaks to anyone concerned about open country. Whatever their stand on our state's growth management policy, few of my neighbors speak well of the exurban sprawl that will spell doom around here for walking, pack riding, and other profitless pleasures. They can see Californication transforming the Northwest, and though attendant social problems are blamed on drugs or Latino immigrants, no one protests the vanishing of commons. Yet a recent survey of natural areas in my city turned up so little habitat that members of the environmental commission were reduced to mapping quarter-acre scraps. These may be just sufficient, if luck holds, to provide workfare colonies for cliff swallows. But it remains to see whether our city's largesse will serve other shirkers of the global marketplace. In the absence of vacant lots, our kids, for instance, may have to settle for video games and loud, alienated music— the usual narcotics.

To take an earful of complaint from developers, as our city council does, is to find the terms of scarcity placed otherwise. Unregulated industry, profit margins, and similar abstractions grace the passions of speculators; golf courses and tennis courts are their sacred groves. One local builder of mini malls tried to fulfill a zoning requirement by designating five acres of his parking lot as a categorical "open space." And so, though I haven't sought the company of developers, in my prejudice I suppose them among the first to post their land and among the last to enjoy the virtues of easy rambling. Few people of any sort voice concern for the prospect of walking without having to breast fences, enter binocular range of someone's privacy, or turn tail from the threats of keep-out signs.

Avarice, the desire to keep all the world to oneself, is an everyday sin and one of which I don't pretend ignorance. Yet I've never grasped the stinginess of the American property owner. To care for a thing correctly, shouldn't we *disguise* its value, as brooding killdeer will lead you far from their clutch by feigning injury? If ranchette owners were in step with nature they would sentry a few junked cars by the mailbox. Then, having thrown real evildoers off the scent, they could supplant trespass signs with discrete notices tacked up in the hawthorns: "Walk fifty paces northeast for passage to hills beyond," they might read. "Avoid private residence on left." Instead, how petty our middle-class reflex to deny others a walk in the air. The refusal of rural poor folks is at least more resourceful. They have their avarice both ways, positioning a rustbucket or two among the signs announcing savage dogs. True love of land is seldom seen in the West, but I read of a Michigan man so fond of a certain tree stump on his property he hides its worth from hunters by crowning it with a beer can.

I think it no accident that among traditional Arabs, a woman's unauthorized departure from the home is called "trespass." In thirteenth-century England, the concept of trespass evolved as "a breach of the king's peace." Robin Hood jacklighting deer or picnickers gathering wild thyme must have spoiled many a night's rest for the royal despot, never mind the vast acreage buffering him from such rabble. We Americans have our own notions about land use. If an engine powers your travel, and if you like to imitate the four-wheeler ads, the earth is your sandbox. But going around on foot is an act of sedition.

A friend visiting from Norway observed that the land of the free is not really your land and my land "from California to the

New York Island." Much of it belongs to faceless investors. But even when the land is publicly owned, first served are the well connected and the deep of pocket. At least that's how it looks to Hallvard from Lillehammer. Here in Kittitas County, for example, you cannot travel by leg power in the absence of gas-powered vehicles—not anywhere in the foothills surrounding our spacious valley. On winter ski excursions or summertime walks, whenever we go, we steel ourselves for the company of engines. Hallvard can't believe this state of affairs. "What is so difficult in setting aside some land for others?" he wonders. "And why can't ORVers stay off the two or three restricted trails you do have?" I reason with Hallvard about the power of commercial lobbies. Never mind the study done by Chelan District rangers showing that non-motorized trekkers outnumber their counterparts ten-to-one. In America, Arctic Cat and Yamaha reps promote their machines as a moral prerogative, and if from lack of cash the nature crowd can't compete in the legislature—well, that's free enterprise. Still, Hallvard doesn't get it. He's from a country that never has embraced the concept of trespass. Open land is Norway's national health plan.

Perceiving the commons differently, walkers and ORVers have little to say to each other when they meet in the woods. One of the latter writes to the newspaper libeling the good name of tree huggers, and I know right away he means people I admire, who wear toothpick skis or tote their children in backpacks. Taking the opposite tack, my hiker's guide deplores trailriders for grinding through our forests, "feeling the wind blow in one ear and out the other."

Such is the rhetoric of the public-lands debate. The opposition are cast as elitists, on the one hand, or yahoos on the other. I guess I am an elitist myself if that means preferring clean air, stillness, and unscorched earth. Yet it is a gradual discovery, learning that you belong to this here elite class. Friends of mine have been run off logging roads by non-elitists in $25,000 pickups for the offense of riding $300 bicycles. And if you believe the average snowmobiler will share the trail with skiers, perhaps you are a bureaucrat with the Forest Service.

That is why I was so gratified one day last winter when Hallvard and I took our skinny boards and poles up Table Mountain. I feared he would return to Norway with only the bleakest notions of my countrymen. There we were, pausing in our woolen elf hats while a troop of Lord Vader's minions blew past, when the last rider in their ranks pulled over and idled his engine. "You guys all right?" asked the voice from behind a jet-black mask, expressing surprise at finding people so deep in the woods with only legs for power. It was a small gesture—we told him we were fine—but I valued that moment when suspicion gave way to decency, and I could pretend that such kindness might extend to the land.

On the theory that nice things are nicer than nasty ones, I aspire to good humor, and I prefer to think well of strangers. But telling stories like mine does nothing to foster respect for the earth. When like-thinking people turn their gaze to state and federal holdings—the great public commons—they sober quickly, realizing how much is at stake in their fate. Looking toward the outlying regions of my county, I wonder: are they varied, numerous, and accessible enough to give sensible recreation while encouraging wildlife? Can they serve the physical freedom that is the source and symbol of political liberty?

Three large tracts must answer for Kittitas County. The first, L.T. Murray Wildlife Area, stretches south from Joe Watt Canyon, crosses Manastash Ridge, and borders our city and the national forest. Like many lands under the Fish and Wildlife Department, "the Murray" is heavily grazed, logged, and motorcycle-scarred over much of its terrain. Still, to the walker, this preserve offers glimpses of golden eagles, wintering elk herds, endless prospects on and off trails, and on rare days, a sky full of silence.

Our state park, the Iron Horse, is sown upon a disused section of the Northern Pacific Railroad. As part of the Mountains-to-Sound Greenway project, this commons will stretch from Seattle to Idaho if completed. While walking portions of the Iron Horse trail, however, I have several times made adjacent land owners apoplectic. Inexplicably, some believe that the park constitutes a "takings" by the state. They want taxpayers to compensate them for the injury of public bypass. I try to countenance these would-be toll collectors when we meet, listening quietly, closing cattle gates behind me, damning them to hellfire only in the privacy of my thoughts. In any case, the Iron Horse takes in nothing but the railroad right of way as it passes through farm land, range, alluvial hardwood groves, and the city of Ellensburg. Eastward, it beelines for the Columbia River. You might suppose it the ideal route for a long pilgrimage begun at your doorstep. Yet some have complained that the trail doesn't lead anywhere. Idaho is not Canterbury, nor the holy land for that matter, and once you head out on the Iron Horse there is no other path by which to circle back: travelers can only retrace their steps. However, this feature may generate a connoisseur's appeal. It is stirring to know that when prophets come among us, they can find their way to the desert on foot.

Most widely controversial are the uses of Wenatchee National Forest, which borders the Kittitas Valley in two directions. Property rights groups complain that too much of this land is going to waste, that it should be cut more quickly and thoroughly, and that ultimately, such federal lands should be "returned" to private ownership. They do not, of course, advocate returning these lands to Native Americans. Every generation, the sagebrush rebellion is revived, but it is always about guilding private coffers at public expense, and its posses don't mind refashioning history to justify the theft. In fact, however, when the tribes were forced to cede their territories, the Western states did not exist. One-fourth of the land immediately came under federal ownership— 726 million acres in which every taxpaying citizen now owns a share. These comprise our greatest commons—the national forests, the Bureau of Land Management tracts, the national parks, and the wildlife refuges. Talk of giving it all back to the states is cant. The only land grabs the federal government can be accused of (by whites, anyway) occurs in the chambers of the U.S. Congress. Beneficiaries include realtors, corporate ranchers, and timber and mining executives; their victims are wildlife and the common citizen. As for federal management practice, ecologists have confirmed the obvious. Fire suppression, overcutting, overgrazing, industrial tourism, and gouge-and-run mining have done to the commons what a vivisectionist does to a rat.

I grant that undisturbed pockets remain in Wenatchee National Forest. If you don't mind driving a long way, and if you are neither a child nor an elder but an athlete in the peak of conditioning, you can reach wilderness areas in time to turn around before nightfall. Perhaps the political winds will shift one day, and greenways can bring together towns and wild lands. For now we content ourselves with staving off their loss.

Since the national commons have served industry more reliably than anyone else, the miracle is that any sauntering grounds remain. But when Thoreau foresaw the attack on the commons, he recommended that we "improve our opportunities...before the evil days come." In other words, take a day off and stride into the huckleberries while unconcessioned berrying grounds remain. In my experience, the work of conservation only improves when upheld by good cheer. Let it be the joy of many to scout the commons and sing their praise.

A friend of mine from Oxford, meanwhile, sings elegies. He sent me this verse protesting developments that threaten Port Meadow:

> The fault is great in man or woman
> who steals a goose from off the common,
> but what can plead that man's excuse
> who steals the common from the goose?

Beyond the keep-out signs, beyond the sell-out of public lands, the promise of common ground remains. It is the promise of Woodie Guthrie's refrain, "This land was made for you and me." Rambling a stretch of Umtanum Ridge the other day, as blind to possession as the stones underfoot, I listened for that affirmation. To walk in its spirit was to reclaim liberty. As free people, let those who care speak a word for the commons.

The Kittitas Rip

As MONTHS OF the year go, April gets more than a passing nod from English-speaking poets. I don't know why that should be except that spring is known for windiness, a quality that good poets avoid. There's T.S. Eliot, who wrote at great length and in low spirits about April, but he was one to lace his wingtips ever so tightly. "What are the roots that clutch, what branches grow / out of this stony rubbish?" he asks dejectedly. For answer we might turn to Robert Frost, who spent his Aprils clomping around in mud and giving sermons about the work ethic. "Only where love and need are one, / and the work is play for mortal stakes, / is the deed ever really done," he opines, and he may be right, though his judgment sounds tinny when read out of season. Then again we have Geoffrey Chaucer, who spoke kind words about the fourth month. Fond as he was of banter and fireside yarns, this poet knew what to do with blustery weather—take a walk in good company.

Well, here in the second week of April, the weather that's galloping overhead from west to east has knocked the whole Columbia Basin on its backside. Gale-force wind scatters everything not bolted down and drives herds of cumulo-stratus clouds before it in a panic. Out where I live the flight patterns of courting snipe appear even more erratic than usual, while in town, people on the streets look shaken. "It's horrible! It's *literally* irritating!" one survivor called above the roar to me. "Gets my goat," said another. The most confusing report involves a bug-eyed librarian who left her west-lying home in Cle Elum this morning, but was seen beating a retreat toward Badger Pocket—that's *east* of here—at quitting time.

I don't know if she meant to obey Chaucer's example. We tried to follow it, my young son and I, by walking the quarter mile to our mailbox and back. Halfway there, two-year-old Erik fronted the breeze, and raising both hands overhead, shouted, "Stop, wind!" But it didn't stop, not any more than it stopped when Xerxes ordered his soldiers to bullwhip the waves of the Hellespont.

Forces we call "elemental" outmuscled even the Persian emperor. The westerlies that visit their spunk upon our region come from way out in Pacific waters, drenching the Puget Basin en route and sucking dry every drop to spare here in the Cascade rain shadow. They scatter the seed of weeds and flowers in their gustings, so that pollination and our valley's wealth of herbaceous burrs owe part of their success to wind. On April days you can watch globes of knapweed spinning across the prairie, bringing grief to farmers (who like "clean" fields) and naturalists (who prefer native species). However, when milkweed pods and dandelions mature, the young at heart will commit their own breath to seed dispersal. It might take a poet to say so, but child's play proves that we belong here in nature, just as the wind itself.

Before I take another walk in an April wind, I will surrender all resistance. Tolerance can begin with familiarity despite the proverb, and a prevailing, thirty-five-mile-an-hour gale deserves a name. I have felt the teeth of the Foehn in Austria, the Rocky Mountain Chinook, the Bungay Jar in New Hampshire, and New England's Montreal Express, too. Out of respect for my adopted home, I greet the Kittitas Rip.

Part IV

Arbor Day

BUYING A HOUSE, they say, is like getting married upon short acquaintance. When we bought ours, Lori and I had more cause for self-reproach than many. After all, the property's post-honeymoon qualities were obvious by the time we reached the altar, which is to say, the real estate office. Our new place was treeless. It offered six acres of Washington prairie and lots of wholesome thistleweed, but not a sapling or twiggy eminence in view. The house had stood for twenty years, itself preceded by an earlier dwelling on the site. What phobias, we wondered, had kept that little farmyard bare? What negligence made for this leafless home? At the same time I thought, could the error of perception belong to me who sought to alter a landscape naturally sparse?

Arbor Day this year found me shovel in hand, and all the warrant I needed for my task was this: Russian thistles being no more native to the area than sassafras, I might as well think my thoughts in the shade. Besides, I argued to anyone who would listen, we will plant trees that are drought resistant. No lush-leafed growth for us; instead, the twisted bark of the naturalized black locust, its channels and grooves puckered with thorns like the devil's hangnails and overhung with seedpods that would poison a ditch-dwelling carp. We could take comfort in knowing our plantings might survive us, as azalea bushes would not. Besides, in a country where ranchers routinely chain-drag the steppes to remove native growth, I would take vengeance by planting cottonwoods and willows. But at the local nursery my intentions were lost in translation. I came home with the makings of an oak bower.

The next day I gave my spade to the job of welcoming the new saplings home. My task consisted mostly of clearing potato-sized rocks from hard clay, scutwork unless you inhabit the late twentieth century and make your living in a climate-controlled office. In that case, outdoor work is the life of Reilly. You can spend a Saturday grunting and sweating, and you can feel the wing of a turkey vulture sweep the ground, but you'll be pleased in a liberatingly witless way. While I sweated and grunted, I resumed the debate about landscape and appropriate species. "If you were an oak tree," I wondered, "would you live here?"

"We *are* oak trees, and you have given us no choice," I answered for the saplings, since trees will speak only to the pure in heart. "But at least we are Garry oaks," they continued, "native to the Northwest, where once we grew in wide savannahs beloved by deer and frequented by hunters with stone-tipped arrows."

My conversation with the trees took root from there. I learned that shallow, rocky soils are fine for the long-lived Garry oak. I discovered that one mature tree can bear eighty-five pounds of acorns in a year, and that if mine ever do so while I'm alive, I can watch for the company of woodpeckers and band-tailed pigeons, not to mention mule deer and countless rodents of every inclination. Furthermore, acorns that don't get eaten will bring new oaks from the ground, for they need but 10 percent surface contact to germinate. And any nuts that fail to sprout will still be rolling and crunching underfoot months later, the "old maids" or confirmed bachelors of their crop who find sport at last in the hands of sharpshooting children with a penetrating need to shatter plate glass.

So, as in marriage, we justify our land-use practices in hindsight and give our hearts to the upshot with a will.

Green Man

"THE STORY OF Johnny Appleseed is true, whether it's true or not," my wife confides, and I believe her. In school we learn of the selfless orchardist, a wayfaring pilgrim of the outback who seeded the frontier with apple trees. Messenger, woodsman, friend to wounded birds, he would have been necessary to invent had he not existed.

From where Lori and I stand in a tightly managed plantation of Wenatchee National Forest, we can see row upon row of identical, thirty-year-old ponderosas, bristling like a Macedonian phalanx. We feel it is right to invoke the memory of someone who cared for trees.

John Chapman was what the English call a green man. Green men live at the margins of settlement and wild country. Part gamekeeper, part herbalist, part gnome, the green man is every land's protector. He knows the properties of leaf mold, and he vanishes before the bulldozer. But even after his groves are felled, the Pan-like faces of green men sprout from cornices on banks and gothic cathedrals. Green women, or wiccans, are their counterpart—in history they've ministered to abandoned wives and been burned at the stake for loving nature better than they loved the county governors.

Took Rafferty, the green man of my home town, lived in a trailer next to a swamp that inexplicably we called "the sandpit." He kept a lot of dogs in grub and never bathed, but he ran the last trapline for miles around, and he gathered ginseng, wild asparagus, and watercress. Some laughed that Took ate possums and skunk; but as I recall, fruit trees perfumed the air around his dwelling. In speech he sounded biblical and heathen at once. Yet his voice was keyed like a cello. When Took Rafferty disappeared in the flood of 1968, we felt his absence the way you miss an old tree brought down by wind.

John Chapman never visited the Cascades, but surely, the ghost of some Sehaptian speaker haunts the skeleton boughs we are walking under. The piercing call of a Stellar's jay links our senses to his memory and that of the unruly forests he knew. If that man appeared suddenly from the shadows today, I would apprentice myself to him willingly.

Samuel de Champlain alone among European conquerors appreciated green men. Like Columbus and Raleigh before him, he brought Native Americans to court as curiosities. But he also left French boys with the Hurons in Canada to learn *their* languages and ways. When they grew up, those boys became the famous couriers de bois, woodland messengers; and whatever commercial purpose they fulfilled, I like to think Champlain gave them to the Indians for their own sake.

A green man is the spirit of a place, what the Romans called its *genius loci*. If ever the time were ripe to remyth our countryside with green men, that day is here. Who in America has not seen the settings of their life erased, and with them, the sources of themselves? Who has not questioned the cost of transforming the entire natural world in all its complexity into mere property, a vast legal abstraction?

We need new green men and women, farm kids, rucksacking students, any who will give their hearts to nature, so Johnny Appleseed may walk this land again.

Against the Nature of Oates

WHEN A RESPECTED literary artist attacks your cause, you can bristle and chafe, answering kicks with blows, or you can hear the woman out. Joyce Carol Oates thinks nature writing a ridiculous genre and nature writers a drab lot. As for nature itself (which the author keeps in a separate drawer from humankind), "Nature is mouths." She says so in an essay first published in the journal *Antaeus*, which I paused over recently as one might consider a dubious-looking mushroom in the woods. My field guide advises testing fungi by taking a spore print. Although I've read Oates's "Against Nature" several times now, I am not ready to pronounce it edible.

People do rhapsodize about the wild in all facility, often from the safety of their jogging trails. According to Ms. Oates, a running path is the site of her near heart attack some years ago, an experience which produced this epiphany: nature is "completely oblivious to the predicament of the individual." Shame on nature writers, she implies, who don't account sufficiently for cobwebs, biting flies, and corpses in decay. Joyce Carol Oates, on the contrary, offers a fresh view of the subject. She would rather we take a hard-eyed look at the apathy and random terror that nature may inspire. Henry Thoreau got himself one heck of a bride, in her opinion. "Come off it Henry David," she teases, you spent a lot of breath composing pep talks that say how pain and death are trivial in the larger scheme.

To the extent that suffering is real, Oates has a point. Outside the window where I work this morning, a feral cat tears the wing from a house finch and drags it in her mouth while scampering around the victim. It is not a moment for spectating, yet how do I finish off the bird? There is this brass bookend at my elbow, but I dither, not wanting to bungle an act of mercy. Meanwhile, the cat begins to eat the finch headfirst, and I am relieved. Oates is clever enough to catalogue the hideous. Leeches attach themselves between her toes; she cannot tear her eyes away from a raccoon's rabid frenzy. Others who reject nature seem to know so little about it. For the writer Brigid Brophy, nature is acceptable only as scenery and best viewed through the glass of a well-engineered import. But Oates offers the local habitations and the names. Her maggots squirm at the roots of bead lilies, not just in dumpsters. As the narrator in "Against Nature," she assumes an ugly persona, but in the end we are meant to understand that her mask is simply mimetic. After complaining that humans alone use language, she closes the essay by describing an invasion of sugar ants. They foray across the narrator's writing desk, where, it happens, she is straining to complete a poem:

> One by one they appear on the dazzling white table and one by one I kill them with my forefinger, my deft right forefinger, ashing each against the surface of the table and then dropping it into a wastebasket at my side. Idle labor, mesmerizing, effortless, and I'm curious as to how long I can do it, sit here in the brilliant March sunshine killing ants with my right forefinger, how long I, and the ants, can keep it up.

I have pondered this massacre of ants. Looking at nature, an orthodox Puritan sees only evil and so responds in kind. But there is more to Oates's denouement. How does a conscious being respond to indifference, apparently a personal condition, but one also implied to be general? The answer presents itself when, voila, the narrator announces, "I've written my poem." In other words, kill something if you must (insects being so unsingular anyway), swap violence for violence, but at all costs make art. Oates's art is bad for the ants, yet they are insensible to the making of "(VERBAL) LANGUAGE."

Suppose our author embroidered her anecdote. After all, it is a ticklish muse who backs writers into the satirist's corner. Jonathan Swift would be standing with Joyce Carol Oates, but kidding aside, his "Modest Proposal" was an attempt to save lives. She is merely displaying wit, another of the qualities she claims for humankind alone.

My interest in Oates's essay and my doubts about the author's wisdom amount to this: she chose to kill the ants, just as she chose to remember the rabid coon instead of a blooming bower, or more to the point, the full range of relationships going on in such a place. She selected bits to quote from Samuel Johnson, Wallace Stevens, and a half-dozen others, stitched them together with words of her own, then titled and published her piece as an act of intention. Fashioning reality by the same method, I may file my memory of the dying house finch next to the carol of the whipoorwill I heard one midnight in the woods. It was like your first dream in a foreign language—probably concerning the purchase of shoes, but thrilling nonetheless—an unlooked-for blessing. Squatting on a cliff at moonrise, I heard the bird say, "purple wheel," and I saw needles of light outlining the trees.

This is not to pose an existential maxim. I never knew birdsong to staunch the flow of blood. It serves no purpose to visualize Ansel Adams's photographs when the world is burning and the moment demands political action. But still there is choice. In the spirit of Descartes, one may hinge one's life upon that "I" which even Joyce Carol Oates admits is an empty cipher. Buddhists assert that our claimed uniqueness is a fiction, and death, our unspeakable horror, a primer in sanity. I don't pretend to understand these matters fully, but I hear that Buddhist communities, on the whole, have had good dealings with their land. Life in the West permits no end of styles, including artistic conceits that are not much concerned with life giving.

Risking immodesty to say so, my cause is nature. A biospheric chemistry beyond my ken, forests and tundras I've never seen as well as landscapes close to home, the right to healthy habitat of animals, native peoples, and the voiceless of the earth—these receive the surplus of my meager attentions, like the crumbs dropped for songbirds by Wordsworth's Cumberland beggar. I appreciate the odds opposing cultural reform, and as an English teacher, the unlikelihood of reforming minds with books. Yet the flag that I salute shows the water planet, and its standard bearers make words: Thoreau, Muir, Leopold, and Austin; Carson, Olson, and Abbey; Snyder, Berry, Lopez and Silko; Zwinger, Pyle, and Tempest Williams. These are my personal canon of nature writers and, I believe, great hearts, though Oates accuses them of fraud. Nature, she says, "inspires a painfully limited set of responses in 'nature writers'—REVERENCE, AWE, PIETY, MYSTICAL ONENESS." She puts them in the same league as evangelicals who parrot a shopworn text. Their enthusiasm must appear ludicrous to grown-ups.

I admit this much: it is not easy to write a compelling narrative about your experience camping beneath an osprey's nest. Ask any writer who's tried it. The osprey may have shown no more than a feather tuft. Even so, unlike indoor literati, nature writers must report the facts as they find them. Real landscapes resist the projection of heroic egos. Strange to say, this inclusiveness may explain the rise of popular interest in nature writing. But fresh-air excursions are only the most obvious feature of this genre. Riches of description and speculative musing embellish nature books. Their grounding in science is solid. As a reader, I claim for them a full range of emotion, and if they sound apostolic to Ms. Oates, at least they are calling for life in *this* world. Pie in the sky is a dish for those who sever us from the rest of nature, which

Oates dismisses for containing "no symbolic subtext—excepting that provided by man." If nature writers want to convert us, is it because the things they defend are all we can know? Conventional wisdom (and that of Oates) holds that the sane mind produces hackneyed art. If so, we may choose as we like.

But let's at least be informed. For topical range, we can try the volume *Refuge,* by Terry Tempest Williams. Its chapters chronicle fluctuating water levels in the Great Salt Lake, nuclear testing in the desert, the vanishing of native birds, and the succumbing to breast cancer, one by one, of women in the author's family. A more recent essay by Williams contrasts pornography's arid climes with the erotic qualities of a healthy landscape. Surely it is this author's talent to forge unlikely alliances in subject matter, but consider the upshot, a nature story for adults.

If whimsy is wanted, there's Barry Lopez. Following clear to the South Pole history's chatter of nationalistic teeth gnashing, he recounts how Amundsen and Scott planted flags when they came, cursed the wind, and left. Traveling to that icy reach himself, the narrator launches a paper kite. And yes, what about dramatic irony? We can read Gretel Erlich dreaming of a teenaged cowboy she'd turned away from her bed one time, who is now freshly dead while spring rages through Wyoming and "sap rises in obdurateness." For humor, my favorite is Edward Hoagland: "A turtle is like a bird with the governor turned low."

Maybe taste defines quality. We admire what we find becoming. And so, as surely as some books are to sample and some are to swallow whole, "Against Nature" is prose best left on the plate. We can still hope that Oates's heart is on the mend.

Green Teens

A MISTY MORNING in April finds twenty teenagers planting
fir trees, laying down riprap for trout, or pulling dis-
carded Big Gulp cups from a stream they call "Xanthus"
after a river god in ancient Ionia. They are the Environmental
Club of our local high school, and their example brightens a dark
time.

Since its founding a half dozen years ago, the club has been
handed down like an heirloom, a class gift that each year attracts
a fuller diversity of membership than school groups peopled by
future farmers or business leaders. A list of the Environmental
Club's recent doings sounds like the report of a U.N. development
agency. Besides hosting field studies with professionals, nature
hikes with teachers, and a visiting speakers program, the club has
participated in a Yakima River clean-up day, planted over 500
trees, initiated paper recycling on campus, and carried off a
home-room competition to encourage commuting to school on
foot or bicycle. For Earth Day this year, the Club planned a full
schedule of assemblies and contributed to our city's festival as
well. As members of the state-sponsored Adopt-a-Stream program, they have designed a future community garden—or perhaps a children's playground; they're not sure yet—at the site of
an erstwhile neighborhood dump along the Xanthus.

Our green teens defy the trademarks of Generation X, and
they do so in a spirit of innocence. I ask a group of them why they
give their time to the earth instead of, say, going shopping. Au-
rora replies that the land is her connection to childhood, and she
doesn't want to lose either one. Maryanne, an exchange student
from Germany, believes that the environment is at the core of
every crisis and is the basis for solving all human problems. Alex

allows that it is possible to change, if not human nature, then each person one by one. Such changes have occurred when apathetic peers have suddenly, like jack-pine seeds exposed to flame, been sparked to life by club-sponsored events. Likewise, Leslie recalls nature's power to bring people together. On picnics and camping trips she has felt herself giving up distractions, acquiring only peace and a sense of community.

"Then how do you feel," I next ask the Club members, "about the recent study which finds that merely 8 percent of American adults consider nature a relevant topic, while 90 percent of American children do?" Their answers come swiftly: "Kids are less in denial than adults"; and, "Adults care about costs; kids care about what's right." Clearly, I thought, these young people are not tiny children, yet like children they keep their windows open. The Powers that Be can see through a glass but darkly.

How do Club members maintain good cheer when all around them politicians are smashing environmental laws like skinheads on a spree? "It's painful to stay focused," says Leslie, "but you have to think yourself through it and not give up." Says Alex, "Nature itself is the source of hope. If changing the way we live makes so much sense—I don't see how it can't work!"

Personally, I don't see how in good conscience we can dismiss the hope of young people like Alex. They are the new growth on our blighted, national terrain.

Morels

RELIABLE SOURCES held that in a nearby canyon thickly wooded with second-growth Doug fir and pine, morel mushrooms might be ripe for the plucking. It was the season of spring when larches needle out, when balsamroots and lupines celebrate their prairie life—the time when evergreen forests yield the mushroom-lover's choicest quarry. As I wheeled my bicycle into a sapling grove, I pictured a frypan sputtering with morels in the company of garlic and red pepper rounds. Or better still, a campfire meal and the spark of enthusiasm that comes from eating wild food outdoors. What more could anyone want?

Like any mountain glen in May, this one flowed musically with run-off, and the sound of snowmelt coursing over rocks helped me to walk with unaccustomed stealth. I watched an ouzel weiring in a pool and a pair of myrtle warblers mating from branch-end to branch-end of an alder thicket. Around a bend in the rocks I surprised a coyote in the act of drinking, its pink tongue slapping the shallows like a salmon's tail. Underfoot, fresh growth nubbled through duff and leaf litter. Yet it was all so verdant and photosynthetic, not a mushroom in sight.

Mushroom seekers learn to ignore the color green. To find what I'd come looking for, I needed to recalibrate my vision. Like many people, I'm drawn to anything vividly hued, color being a sure sign of fruit to our jungle-dwelling ancestors. Hence the appeal of wildflowers. But a mushroom is the pallid body of a fungus and the means by which the unseen, subterranean plant can reproduce. It's ugly by the standards we apply to other vegetation. Mushrooms also differ in lacking chlorophyll: instead of converting sunlight to food, they extract their nutrients from living roots—some through an elegant symbiosis—or else, like the black morel, by breaking down rotten wood and other dead material. All mushrooms perform the dirty work of energy exchange, appearing suddenly, feeding the forest, growing as clumps, brackets, or fairy rings, then vanishing completely. In ancient Greece they sprang up in the wake of Zeus's lightning. In the Middle Ages, "little people" danced under toadstools at midnight. Native Americans and hippies have borrowed the visionary verve of some species, calling *Psilocybes* "the food of the gods."

On the other hand, Death Cap amanitas have destroyed the kidneys of unwary gatherers, and Corpse Finders have been discovered growing from human remains, in one case from a box containing a baby's bones. Like anything mysterious in the natural world, mushrooms arouse mixed feelings. In his late etchings, Francisco Goya placed them among the familiars of a black Sabbath, and some people react to them with a visceral loathing. More typically, though, we now find boletes, truffles, and chanterelles selling for eight dollars a pound in markets. Northwest forests crawl with pickers at morel time, and then again during the longer mushroom season in fall. At least one case of manslaughter has been attributed to trespass on somebody else's gathering grounds.

On the day of my search, I found that overgrown canyon terrain compresses time and distance. You can pass a full morning moving several stone-throws, especially when on the lookout for elusive prey. My eyes combed surfaces varied by texture, light, and depth of field, so that after a while, forms appeared to separate and then to regroup. Stream bed gravel merged with the water above it, and that in turn with branches of the canopy reflected in its own still pools. Pieces of interwoven sky fed yet another dimension of data to my overloaded optic nerves. Hunters must know the dizziness that comes from concentration. At last you long for an opening.

Mine came when the woods broke suddenly at the shore of a talus field. Among the rocks, pikas gave their warning calls, while in the distance a pair of jays were dive-bombing an eagle. The larger bird dipped above basalt pillars that gaped like Easter Island effigies. I returned to the woods still wedded to pursuit, this time crawling on knees and elbows under a screen of branches. Like birth and death, mushrooms thrive on dark and wet. Here, in this obscure pocket near the source of Reecer Canyon, I thought I might find morels at last. Plenty of dead wood lay scattered about beneath the firs. There was even evidence of burning in the soil. But the only fungi I could see were inedible polypores staircasing up a tree trunk. I rested on a corky log.

As children we are told many parables of desire, and while my vision of sautéed morels began to fade, I thought about "The Fox and the Grapes," "The Fisherman's Wife," and my late grandmother's wish to be spoon-fed chocolate mousse on her deathbed. Oh, the power and the weakness of wanting. It sets the seeker on his path, and if the saints tell truly, defeats him. I pondered the lore of mushrooms, whose paths are underground. Expanding the roots of trees in exchange for carbohydrates, they give as the condition of getting. Meanwhile, at my feet, another presence shifted into focus: a pale-green lily, tiny, and evidently modest in its needs, a flower I had never seen before and as it turned out, one I haven't been able to find in any field guide.

Back-country Time

i.

THIS IS THE SEASON when summer stays, when you and your partner will gaze over evening grass and thunder-heads as corn shoulders up in lots around the canning plant—the wealth of prairies piled for towns—when breezes fan the garden and green shade trees provide. In August you both feel pleasantly belated. Nostalgia ripens like the vine as you pick over memories of summer days when summer days outlasted your intentions. An August sunset holds no suspense but is suspended, a stasis point in the calendar when it seems that everything living might exist on air.

In the morning, field crickets, ryegrass, the zodiac walking on a slant of light. Close your eyes when sunrise breasts those eastward reaches and listen to swallows twittering in the eaves. A semi downshifting in the distance warrants no more concern than the tiny agitation of flies. Zephyrs twirl a locust pod across the gravel at your feet, a sound like fingernails on seashell. A rooster crows distantly; the scale of the land pygmies even this coxcomb's self-importance. Horses clipping awns are a comfort and a grace. You let yourselves love the morning now. Even with autumn holding its mirror to the earth, you love the infant day. Let everything come to dust, as it will: "death is the mother of beauty."

The liquid rill of a meadowlark quickens the moment, a throaty waterfall. Wind in the willows almost overlays a passing jet's drone. Commuters whisk along the highway a mile to the west, high-speed rubber buffing macadam. A lithe cat leaps at flicking grasshoppers, soundless but for the pressure of her paws meeting. Killdeer paint the meadow shades of one pure emotion, which you understand in human terms as plaintiveness. Other aircraft crowd the audiosphere. A tiny Cessna; a helicopter on fire lookout. Somewhere beyond the scope of hearing, flames kindle in timber. Back here, quail are calling, "Cui-da-do! Cui-da-do!" and your translation is apropos—contentment is a gift to take care of.

ii.

It is time to be leaving. Weeks and months ago you sealed this envelope of time and mailed it to yourselves at a portable address without a zip code. Now, turtlebacked beneath your packs, your sleeping bags and cook-stove piled high, you and your partner hold it in your hands again. When you cross the pass where a rustic sign reads, "Wilderness," you reach for its contents with every footfall.

On back-country time, you look to recapture a primitive Eden in the places you will see. Lost to the world in a mountain range of North America, you may choose at last what becomes you. At the moment it becomes you to attend to other lives. On the talus reaches above Teanaway, the squeeze-toy "eenk" of the pika, and higher still, the drop-jaw shriek of the whistle pig (or hoary marmot), are heard. Then, when you switchback through a bowl, a colony of bog gentians appears among the goldenrods and frost-killed leaves where once in high summer the hawkweed bloomed. A pattern of twigs in a pine grove is art; this dry creek bed, a garden. On back-country time, the corky plates of a fir trunk hold you motionless in the deeper woods—in them you seem to see a face from long ago, an old woman that held your cheeks between her palms when you were young. She gave you dollar bills and praise, but the living tree gives her back to you for nothing.

Now a nurse log carpeted with moss and nurturing young evergreens, a stony field of lichen pods as red as poppies on the far plains of far La Mancha—is this the right place, you wonder, where your final days should deliver you to lie down at last and rise up in life-affirming soil? It was the deathbed of a deer; you finger a flute-like tibia, running your fingers in the cleft where calcium-seeking rodents have gnawed.

On back-country time, a Clark's nutcracker sways from a branch end. Fixing your partner with one black eye, how little he resembles the swallows that live near home, for whom people are slalom gates; or the townie crows and starlings that note you as a face in the crowd. This unforward but curious bird seems to say, "Well, here is a creature worth inspecting." You know that regard this frank is the grace of uncommon hours.

On back-country time, you learn while making tea that a watched pot will boil. Meanwhile, you feel that eyes are looking at you from somewhere in a leafy thicket; so you turn around and turn again to see, until one of those times a coyote scrams the moment you've placed her presence. Later, when your bag of donuts turns up missing from camp you tell yourself, "No, it is not the meek who will inherit the earth, but the supple and the quick to learn."

At last, some days or weeks into the woods, you follow a sunbeam's trajectory beyond all the purposes that wait for you at home. Under the spell of the outer world, you have seen time bait its hook with people's lives. You have measured the odds that favor death to the spirit. But here today you discover a shrine where two great firs embrace a granite boulder. Pausing, you pile small stones into a cairn, for out of humanness you need to comment; you've yearned all along to say how good this world can be, how wonderfully everything belongs together.

You are in the back-country now.

iii.

Real life is not waiting around some corner. Your world as you find it is all there is. What do you listen to? What do you see? It will not take long before places cohere in their particulars and time is on your side again. Even a day hike in the forest can escape the contours of the car ride that brought you. Suddenly, as long as you can remember, you will have been walking through this meadow with a loved one, watching waist-high stalks of hardhack tickling her elbows. In your nose these planty blossoms may yield an underlying sweetness. It will become your whole world, this forever of deep woods thimbleberry bowers, this devil's club lily, and overhead the sweep of cedar fronds will remind you that time runs down but not for now.

Back home you will bring the spirit of the back country, telling your child you're so truly glad he was born, wrapping your arm around his grandmother, finding your place between them. The ghost of the time and the power of place have conspired, you might as well add, for the family to which you all belong is larger than you ever dreamed possible, more intimate, inclusive, and well.

Valley Walking

I see men as trees, walking.
—Mark 8:24

WHILE GROWING up in New England, teenage friends and I liked to imagine our walks as the force behind planetary rotation. As we shuffled down to the covered bridge to smoke joints or climbed through foxtail grass in Slough's Pasture, our myth held that the work of pedestrians stewarded the earth along its orbit.

"I have walked myself into my best thoughts," said Kierkegaard, "and I know of no thought so burdensome that one cannot walk away from it." If he was right, then we can shed anxiety like snakeskin. A good walk conditions the hide. Indeed, people who walk a lot are supposed to enjoy longevity and rude health. Henry Thoreau died of tuberculosis at forty-four, but it is also true that among the last words spoken by the prophet of environmentalism were "moose" and "Indians," themselves outstanding walkers. Asked whether he had made his peace with God, Thoreau replied that no quarrel had parted them. He must have died well, for as they say in Tibet, it is better to live one day as a tiger than a thousand years as a sheep.

Exuberance being our proper destiny, who can miss the significance of Chinese footbinding? For social control of women it was unrivaled; as a mark of the human spirit, purely evil. Fortunately, walking is no longer limited to foot traffic. The State of Washington offers more than a hundred miles of trail suitable for wheelchairs. Though their means may vary, walkers are known by an eager countenance.

The English travel writer, Bruce Chatwin, reported that nomad tribes he lived with were remarkable for the contentment of their children. Bedouin babies rarely cry, and their toddler siblings are seldom given to whining or complaint. His observation rings true—any parent knows that infants can't tolerate stasis. What if migration turned out to be the vehicle of human happiness? My wife thought to test this hypothesis by extending her daily walks while pregnant. From the first week after my son's birth, I, too, walked him for miles in the countryside near our home, hoping to pattern Erik's breath after the rhythm of my stride. That way, when he gained his legs he would be trailbroken. We can claim only mixed results four years later, but similar experience among friends has not stemmed the tide of paperback advice on hiking with kids.

How does it go on a good day? Lori, Erik, and I paused recently at the fork of two paths above Reecer Canyon. "Sorry I could not travel both and be one traveler," I suggested the low road. It curved like a question mark between blonde hills and sidled down into folds of fir and pine, the trees themselves girdled with elderberry, creambush, and hawthorn. The path next regained its footing on the steppe a mile beyond. What lay between we intended to learn.

Minutes of loose-limbed jaunting brought us into the greenery. Among the sagebrush of central Washington, such an oasis of vegetation permits intimacies that take you aback. The wind that had sucked our voices was suddenly stilled. Yarrow and mullein edged our path. Lori split a stalk of the latter weed, and out sprang tiny thrips. Willow shrubs and aspens no bigger around than thumbs kept company by a streambed. Ancient apple trees hunkered among the wilder growth, and from the upper story of the conifers, Douglas squirrels chanted abuse. The ground was scattered with their cone shanks, shorn like corn cobs on a dinner plate.

Since children take poorly to walking on an epic scale, we resolved to spend the afternoon restfully. From the comfort of our lunch log, Erik stuck to close observation of the facts. Like a ground-scratching songbird, he would nibble crumbs of sandwich, creep away to poke at a beetle, then return for another bite. Long views meant nothing to him, so we walked on again, naming what we could see and hear close by. Grasshoppers tickered in the knapweed, spread their red wings and flew. A flicker hammered at the trunk of a ponderosa. Let others praise peaks, we thought. Our hearts will find ease among the coulee crops, the limber and the low.

Toddler outings would satisfy more dependably, I am convinced, if one were not so predisposed to adventure. As it is, I live near mountains, and like many others, I place a certain value on thrill seeking. Lori calls it "batchechism" in tribute to the hormonally inspired. But ever since Petrarch climbed Mount Ventoux in 1336 (the first time any European scaled an Alp for the view), Westerners have sought the dramatic. Polar exploration and child rearing are poorly matched pursuits, however. As a parent, I steep myself in vicarious callings.

For example, in Larry McMurtry's novel, *Streets of Laredo*, we meet a peripatetic character named Famous Shoes. He is an aging Kickapoo Indian who's outlived most of his tribe, one of the many displaced persons wandering McMurtry's brutal West at the close of frontier days. But Famous Shoes has a talent. It saves his life on many occasions, and to my mind, makes him a figure worth emulating. Famous Shoes can *walk*—endlessly, tirelessly, to any destination, living off the land's chance pickings as he goes, and moving swiftly in a steady trot that riders on horseback cannot keep pace with. In one of the novel's most absorbing episodes, Famous Shoes gets up one morning and takes a five-month walk. Starting in northern Mexico, he decides to seek the place where the great flocks of migrating shorebirds go to mate. So he walks the Great Plains bottom to top. He crosses the rivers Red and Platte and Missouri. He enters the forest of the Canadian Shield as shadows lengthen toward fall, arriving finally in a land where the trees stand only as tall as himself. Beyond, he can see no trees at all. The Arctic, McMurtry tells us, seems to Famous Shoes to be the edge of the world. "Overhead, the sky was thick with ducks and geese, going to the place Famous Shoes wanted to go." But winter comes on, and Famous Shoes circles for home. After all, the narrator comments, "he was only a man, of the earth and not of the sky, and his skills were not the skills of birds."

I have been thinking about Famous Shoes because, like many a son of civilization, I feel so alarmingly housebound. We work in brick-and-mortar termite mounds. We imitate travel in speeding cars and airplanes. We do our duty to spouse and children and economic growth. But sometimes I'd like to vanish over a hill. Some people appear content to take the air in short puffs. I watch a local woman running cross-lots every morning while I'm just brewing coffee. From the prospect of my kitchen window, her white ankles flash above the bitterbrush and old cattle ribs where Bone Hill saddles up to Bare Hill. Later in the day, I've watched that same woman emerge unfazed by eight hours inside an office. In our time, this is how active people live. They get by on a diet of weekend outings.

I prefer overnights in the deep woods, passages of at least a week or so, for the same reason that I'd rather stand waist-deep in brambles than fuss over potted plants. But such freedom grows harder to arrange. We have replaced the horse of the West with the highway, as three centuries ago, the horse replaced the Pueblo runner. The true heirs of Famous Shoes, whoever they are, will have to forgive my clinging to middle-class comforts, my family, and my job. But I will be watching with appreciation for the woman or the man like that old Kickapoo, who "left when he felt like leaving, and told no one where he was going or when he might return." Says McMurtry, "There was no confining the man."

Not all walkers escape convention, but many are inspired in one way or another. The writer John Hanson Mitchell, who walks a patch of woods thirty miles from an East Coast city, speaks of meeting a man there dressed in wild animal skins. The rustic confides that he has subsisted for seven years by hunting and gathering, and he invites the author to his cave for home-made birch beer, a mile and several centuries back of the nearby franchise strips. Mitchell reports another vision that appeared to him deeper in the woods: the figure of an old woman in a print dress, her gray hair tied in a bun, who clutched an enormous white rabbit to her breast. She and Mitchell exchanged long looks, and then the woman strode off into the hobblebushes, as errand-sure as a coyote.

Yet it is hard to make a good story from the habit of walking, for unlike big-game hunters, walkers enact no metaphor of amorous pursuit. Nothing much happens while walking besides the changing of the landscape as you roll along. Maybe two roads diverge in a yellow wood and the narrator chooses one rather than the other; or a bird lights down on a branch end only to flit away. A central feature of walking essays is often the writer's emotions, which explains why Emerson's have sedated so many American literature students. Today, educated people both walk less and read less than Emerson (another reason for collegiate narcolepsy). The recent enthusiasm for walking tales is therefore surprising. A good metropolitan book store will feature scores of titles under the category of Nature/Environment, and huge numbers of them are about somebody wandering around outdoors observing plants and animals.

English writers, like English people in general, have often been superb walkers. William Wordsworth is said to have walked over fifty thousand miles during the course of his career. Even Jane Austin, the novelist of high tea and wallpaper, manages to bundle her characters outdoors for a cross-country ramble now and then. With its generous network of public paths, England far surpasses the U.S. as a walker's destination. The British Isles have no mountains or wilderness areas to compare with ours. But their pastoral hills bring contentment to a people avid for whimsical pleasures.

Both suicide and posted property isolate their agents. Only one is illegal, but given sufficient care, transgression may be as hard to prosecute in the second case as in the first.

According to Pascal, "Our nature lies in movement; complete calm is death." Yet the practice of religion, as I understand it, is to achieve repose. Of the two main schools of Buddhism, "the Wide Path" and "the Narrow Path," only the former advocates walking meditation. Followers of the Narrow Path confine their practice to sitting. Which of the sects has been successfully transplanted in North America? Mahayana, the Wide Path. Wallace Stevens seems to sponsor the Mahayanist approach when he writes, "In my room, the world is beyond my understanding: But when I walk I see that it consists of three or four hills and a cloud."

Notwithstanding a bias toward friends and kin, trees are my favorite mortals. They practice quietism, but unlike the preacher of Ecclesiastes, they are not depressed. Most trees droop only when snowed upon. Even their boughs tend upward. A favorite walking sport of my youth was birch bending in the manner described by Robert Frost. You wait until spring, select a youngster with the girth of your two hands' circumference, and shinny up. The trick is to launch outward when gravity makes its pitch. Hesitating, you hang suspended, splayed and ridiculous, as a schoolteacher once hung me looped by my belt to a coat rack.

To know a trail, you have to follow where it leads. Maps cannot guide you to what matters in a walk any more than dogma can settle the question of an afterlife. William Blake: "Improvement makes straight roads; but the crooked roads without improvement are roads of genius." In *The Complete Walker*, Colin Fletcher follows crooked roads, telling us that elk and wild horses blaze the most reliable ones. From the standpoint of a human lost in the outback, deer perform nearly as well, whereas bighorn sheep are "next door to useless." All, it seems to me, make first-rate teachers, however. Tracking them alertly helps us to learn the kinds of country we drive through in cars, and it proves that native skills survive for those with time to hone them. That, unfortunately, is the rub.

Thoreau's favorite synonym for walking was "sauntering." He traced the origin of this word to the time when medieval pilgrims took long journeys to shrines in Palestine. Such travelers were said by the French to be going "*a la Sainte Terre*," to the Holy Land. "There goes a Sainte-Terrer," or saunterer, they would say.

Forty bones uphold the human foot. Given the usual pace of evolution, even the sit-down habits of life nowadays won't fuse these bones any time soon. With luck—and some radical reforms—we could walk the good earth for ages.

On Stuart with Mountain John

ALONG THE TRAIL that will bring me to the highest summit visible from my home, I met a man who spoke of honey trees, wore a beard he might have copied from Charles Darwin, and grew excited about carnivores and the lupines growing on Jolly Mountain.

That was yesterday, so I'll come back to my acquaintance in a moment. Today I am climbing Blue Jay Topknot, an immense granite peak so named by Sehaptian speakers, now titled on maps after a defunct house of Scottish royalty. I like to call Mt. Stuart by its Indian name because it does resemble a jay's feathered crest, and the alternative was coined by General George McClellan, who almost lost the Civil War for the Union. With me today, in spirit at least, is McClellan's younger contemporary, John Muir. My favorite book by the pioneer conservationist, *The Mountains of California*, will not help me to scale a Mt. Stuart palisade or to chimney out of a cul de sac, but reading passages now and then will color my thoughts with those of a man I admire. No technical climber, I—just a scrambler with aspirations. Yet I would carry the colors of John Muir if I could.

From its base in the forested Ingalls Valley to its summit just shy of 10,000 feet, Mt. Stuart is a vertical world. Those who would follow in the footsteps of Muir must learn to dance with gravity. Very soon my body reaches for that axis known as the angle of repose, where climber and mountain meet in what feels this bright morning like an embrace. Above the angle of repose, an object at rest will tumble. Below it, that object being myself, I will merely feel the blood drumming at my temples as the slope reaches into space. I will consider how the fluid within my Eustachian tubes addresses itself to the face of the mountain. I take

my first breather where a couloir opens to a broad slope of talus
and patchy snow, and I read about Muir's ascent of the Nisqually
Glacier on Mt. Rainier.

> When I saw its magnificent moraines extending in majestic curves
> from the spacious amphitheater between the mountains, I was ex-
> hilarated with the work that lay before me. It was one of the golden
> days of summer, when the rich sunshine glorifies every landscape
> however rocky and cold. The path of the glacier was warm now,
> and shone in many places as if washed with silver. The tall pines
> growing on the moraines stood transfigured in the glowing light.

Passion is Muir's authorial lubricant, or as critics have said, his
vice. Reading the chapter on glaciers while climbing Mt. Stuart, I
find the man's optimism infectious. So what if his prose is ba-
roque? Having spent about 30 percent of the 1870s beyond the
angle of repose, John Muir earned whatever excessive happiness
he might be accused of.

On the move again, I set my feet and hands deliberately, but
rockfalls begin to dog my progress. I am well above timberline.
Looking down and seeing how far the stones I kick loose can
tumble is not the way to maintain composure. To banish the jit-
ters I think about breathing. It is safe to assume that mountain
climbing is arduous, but the challenge for me lies not so much in
summoning strength as in paying close attention. Moment by
moment, climbers judge terrain with the zen-like skill associated
with golf pros. Golfers, however, rely on carts and caddies. They
suffer no vagaries of high-country weather.

However mountaineers compare to linksmen, the most impressive are unconcerned with vanity. Muir cared less for personal bests than for the wildlife of the peaks he loved. His many
books were written for the sole purpose of protecting western
lands. The more attractively he portrayed the wild country, Muir

reasoned, the more it would be visited by ordinary people who would fight to preserve it. It's true that we find no bear attacks or killer avalanches in Muir. But it is also conceivable that without his books, the likes of me would never breathe mountain air. He wore his fame lightly, Mountain John did, and beyond all thought of preservation goals, he counted as a supreme disappointment his failure to talk Ralph Waldo Emerson into sleeping under the stars. "You are a sequoia tree yourself," he is said to have exclaimed. "Stop and get acquainted with your big brothers." Emerson was well into his seventh decade at the time and opted for a hotel, so Muir went tramping in Yosemite alone.

At 8,000 feet I'm snacking on apricots and reading Muir's description of the American dipper, or ouzel, that sprightly grey diver of watercourses:

> No cañon is too cold for this little bird, none too lonely, provided it be rich in falling water. Find a fall, or cascade, or rushing rapid, anywhere upon a clear stream, and there you will surely find its complementary Ouzel, flitting about in the spray, diving in foaming eddies, whirling like a leaf among beaten foam-bells; ever vigorous and enthusiastic, yet self-contained, and neither seeking nor shunning your company.

The passage puts me in mind of Muir himself, and so in turn I muse about the last person I met with on the present excursion. Yesterday morning, ten miles to the west along the Teanaway River's north branch, I was greeted by a energetic-looking woodsman. He wore a green cap, gumboots, and that wild, nineteenth-century beard I mentioned before. He carried a rifle slung over one shoulder and a long-handled spade. An aloof-looking bird dog sniffed at a clump of sword ferns near my feet. "My truck's in the next drainage," he said. "Thought I'd see if I could excavate it." (Earlier, I had stumbled upon an ancient Dodge well-rutted into a slough.) The woodsman's age was anybody's guess—his face looked weather carved. He met my gaze with piercing blue eyes, though, and he moved as a man at home in his body.

"I live two canyons over," he continued. "Go left at the fork and you can circle past my trailer." I didn't know whether to take this as an invitation or merely a statement of fact, so I asked about animals. Did he know who made their homes in the neighborhood and who was passing through? The woodsman gazed at a nearby outcropping that, come to think of it, might have sheltered a bobcat litter.

"I was by here with my dog yesterday morning, just before it got light. Out of nowhere this doe comes running down the trail straight at us. Finally, Blue starts barking and the doe veers off into the bushes." He made an arc with his hand to show how.

"Next thing I see is this cougar tailing after. Blue must have froze, because he wasn't barking any more, and the cougar almost run into us just like the deer."

"Did it see you?"

"It stopped and looked at me for a little while—long tail about as thick as a little kid's arm—then it took off again. The deer probably got away. I was so surprised I forgot I was carrying my rifle." The woodsman pointed to the dust at our feet: "That's his track you're following."

We talked together some more, my new friend saying little of himself but revealing a great deal about wild honey bees and the prospects for this year's huckleberry crop. A half-hour after we parted ways, I discovered the trailer where he must live with his dog. Wood chips littered the clearing, but for a bachelor pad the place was neat. A deerskin hung from pins driven into a lean-to, and a coffee pot rested on a chopping block by the front door. The woodsman himself was absent. I left a warm beer beside his coffee pot and struck out for the trail to Ingalls Valley. Only now, today, at 8,000 feet, does it occur to me that John Muir's spirit watches over these woods. On the move once more, I notice a grasshopper clinging to my shirtsleeve. It wears black and white camouflage, its patterning identical to that of the granite we cling to. I see how it eludes its predators, but how does an insect survive the winds that hammer this peak? Nearby, a ledge is heaped with the provender of a pika. Alder leaves and pearly everlasting comprise the feed of this bunny-like creature. Again I'm amazed—how did alder leaves come to such a height? As Muir was happy to point out, alpine residents are tutors for the proud.

Not far from the summit I meet with fear in the shapes of the mountain: wild, hoodoo rocks and black crags chisel the sky. Despite these spires, or because of them, I feel appalled by the dearth of ground surface here. Below the knife edge I negotiate, ether is all. If you've ever scrambled high routes you can appreciate why John Muir made climbing his religion. Muir saw God's masterwork in the western mountains and was the first white man to scale them for the fun of it. He accepted fear in the conviction that only a loss of faith would make him fall.

I myself can only marvel. Supplied with nothing more than bread loaves, breakfast tea, and a woolen blanket, how many nights did he pass in the snow? How many thunderstorms did he ride out, clinging to the topmost branches of a pine tree? I admire John Muir, but the world at 10,000 feet feels alien to me. I have to talk myself through each maneuver at such a height, and the urge to retreat is gaining force. Finally, as I have done before, I turn around before gaining the true summit of Bluejay Topknot. Perhaps I've pushed the limit of my concentration. Or maybe, like Muir in his later years, I long for the people I've left in the valley. Whatever I go up I must come back down.

Dimmity

IGHTFALL ON THE Kittitas Valley. Watching the sky
darken above a county road, we stretch our eyes to
glimpse thePleiades. Whiskey Dick Mountain rolls
eastward toward the Columbia River. The Cascades edge a band
of coral. Cows bray and killdeer pine on the wing. We hear a great
horned owl calling, "Who's-awake? Me-too." As we kick along,
windfall leaves conjure up odors of baking spice, the cardamoms
and maces found in oak-lined pantries of another time.
Ellensburg's water tower anchors the lowlands in dwindling light.

We are out for stars, Lori and I—not the blinding constellations that shake us from our January torpor, but the mellow lights
of Indian summer. I find the Pleiades at last by squinting in the
direction of Mt. Stuart and tilting my head back. Today they are
known as the star cluster M45, but once, according to legend, they
were nymphs and the progeny of Atlas. Observing them chased
by Orion the hunter, Zeus took pity and turned the Pleiades at
first into pigeons, then later, to keep them permanently from
harm, he made them a constellation. They twinkle faintly without a telescope, but the poet Tennyson saw them "glitter like a
swarm of fire-flies tangled in a silver braid." Five of the seven
daughters show themselves when I look from the corner of my
eye, so elusive they barely admit detection. I'll take my illumina-
tions gladly, however dim. As Emily Dickenson observed, "The
truth must dazzle gradually or every man be blind."

Gradual as any discovery has been my search for untraveled
roads in a world where engines rule. In the typical postmodern
landscape, you have to walk abreast of traffic if you want to walk
at all, your lungs absorbing heavy metals. As for stargazing, fu-
turists declare it is only a question of time before satellites blind

the night sky with soft drink ads. For the present, a walking loop where farmland gives way to sagebrush invites my wife and me, especially in early October when sultry days are numbered. We take the crown of the road for ten minutes before meeting with a pickup. The driver lifts his index finger from the wheel in greeting, a remnant of rural courtesy.

After a mile or so, we turn north onto the creek road. Here, the land's open character disappears for a while, and we stride along between cottonwood rows on Appalachian curves. We notice irrigation ditches drawn down to their cobbles. A few swallows circle. More numerous on this stretch, vehicles of every description whisk along their way. Picking up the pace, we wonder where everybody's going. Night-time claims the upper hand, and new sets of headlights appear each time our eyes have adjusted to darkness.

But a left turn onto gravel eases the crimp from our step. There is a point of critical distance from towns. When I reach it, I feel as though I've redeemed a sore conscience. Perseus and Auriga lie low along the hills. Cassiopeia, the celestial W, glimmers overhead. Ten miles out of town now, a scarcity of houses endows the ones we do see with gratuitous character. I imagine their occupants as sons and daughters of the Homestead Act, even though most commute to work in Yakima and plant more TV dishes than crops. Still, views from the gravel road look long enough to cheat the darkness.

In Wales, evening is called *dimmity*. According to the nature writer Henry Williamson (in his novel *Tarka the Otter*), dimmity is the dusky stretch when "a whiteness drifts above the seer reeds of the riverside"; when "voles are at work, clearing their tunnels"; and when otters can hear the scratching of an owl's talons on the bark of their denning trees. I'm of two minds about twilight. By the reading of my inner clock, dimmity pleases and pains me. First the pleasure: to travel by foot from creek to creek as Lori and I are doing, rolling over the high tablelands where coyotes and badgers den, and at the end of the day to see before us the valley we live in appearing as a new-found world—what beguilement, I would like to know, compares with this?

Ahead of us we see the glow of backyard incinerators on either side of the road. Beyond the three-car garage of a newly constructed ranchette, we hear an engine groaning and the clank of steel on gravel. I think I smell tires burning, but Lori assures me it is common household trash—illegally cremated of course, but perhaps less toxic than rubber. There's nothing like conspicuous waste to summon misanthropy, I say. How well the Kittitas might get on with half as many busy homeowners! Lori reminds me, however, that numbers mean less than attitudes.

"People are flexible. They can change the way they live."

"Sure," I say, "but who's volunteering?"

Around another bend, the laboring machine reveals itself as a backhoe. Under a blaze of outdoor lighting, someone is using it to straighten the creekbed. A mosaic of busted-up concrete lines "corrected" portions of the stream; piles of decapitated hawthorns await burning on the opposite bank. Steelhead fry, now extinct here, will not require their shade. As confirmed ergophobics, who are we to critique such initiative? Does any forum exist for doing so?

At this point I recall an aphorism once shared with us by a friend. When you're fixing on where to settle down, he'd warned us, "Choose for the place, not the people." After all, he explained, people always leave. Ten years later, our friend's remark strikes me as bitterly existential. It was originally delivered in the tone used by a woman I once overheard in an Arizona jukejoint: "Men—

you can't trust any of the bastards." People can be fickle in their loyalties, there's no doubt about that, and as the backhoe driver has just made clear, meddling is the reflex and the curse of our kind. Yet I want to improve my outlook. Cynicism invites paralysis.

"People do leave," Lori says, agreeing with the existentialist. It is her time to take the low road. "And the ones that stay take leave of their senses. Before you know it, places disappear, too. How long will it be before this valley is a wall-to-wall subdivision?"

I let the subject die. I have no answer but to move my legs. We take our long walks as if the habit were a holy office. Yet the shopping malls, storefront realtors, and car wash emporiums are coming, and the inertia driving growth will render our surroundings unrecognizable. For now, as Mars and Venus romance the western sky, I can put off grieving. We hear the trencher cut his engine down along the road behind us, and the darkness is restored to a silence you can breathe. Tonight, at least, we will read dimmity for our bedtime story.

Soon we have completed our circuit. If you follow in our tracks, be sure to stuff your pockets with dog biscuits, and don't mind if hounds pass the word that you're coming. When you reach your doorstep, you can deck the lintel with a chicory sprig. It will not be a political statement, perhaps, but a way of greeting the night sky, star by star.

Acknowledgments

I AM GRATEFUL TO Dale Harrison and Kathleen Trotter of Northwest Public Radio, and to Beth DeWeese and Keith Petersen of WSU Press. Also at WSU Press I would like to thank Tom Sanders, Mary Read, Jean Taylor, Wes Patterson, Sharon White, and Jenni Lynn. I owe more than I can say to my teachers, my family, and the Source.

About the Author

ROBERT SCHNELLE is heard in Washington, Oregon, and Idaho as a commentator on Northwest Public Radio's "Morning Edition." He grew up in small-town and rural New England before moving with his family to Washington's Kittitas Valley. *Valley Walking* is his first book.